ADOPTION
The Grafted Tree

ADOPTION
The Grafted Tree

Laurie Wishard, M.S.W.
William R. Wishard, LL.B.

cragmont publications

Published by
Cragmont Publications
China Basin Building
161 Berry St., Suite 6410
San Francisco, CA 94107

First printing, September, 1979
Manufactured in the United States of America

Editing: Diane Sipes, San Francisco
Cover design: Carolyn Bean Associates, San Francisco
Typography: Medallion Graphics, San Francisco
Printing & binding: Science Press, Ephrata, PA

Library of Congress Cataloging in Publication Data

Wishard, Laurie, 1948-
    Adoption: the grafted tree.

    Includes index.
    1. Adoption—United States.   I. Wishard,
William R., 1930-   joint author.   II. Title.
HV875.W49   362.7'34'0973   79-19368
ISBN 0-89666-006-0 pbk.

Contents

Part II
Acting on the Decision

Part III
Creating the New Family Tree

Part IV
The Search for the Native Tree

Appendix

Acknowledgments

We are indebted to the many birthparents, adoptive parents, adoptees, social workers, attorneys, and foster parents who shared their personal experiences with us. This book is really their story. Thanks are also given to the numerous public and private agencies that readily gave us their assistance, their time, and their knowledge.

We particularly appreciate the assistance of Sister Rosanne Curtis, a Los Angeles adoption social worker. She provided us with invaluable insights into the workings of adoption agencies and into the emotional issues of the adoption process.

Finally, we wish to thank our family. Betty Wishard, particularly, contributed to countless discussions about adoption, our family experiences, and this book.

Other Books by William R. Wishard

Rights of the Elderly & Retired
Credit & Borrowing in Texas
Credit & Borrowing in New York
Credit & Borrowing in Illinois
Credit & Borrowing in Florida

Introduction

All of us have made major decisions in our lives. Usually we decide to leave our parents' home, to earn our living in a certain way, to marry or not to marry, and often to end a marriage or a relationship. These are common experiences but they are unique and personal for each of us. Many of us have made or will make a decision about the adoption of a child. There are approximately two and one quarter million adoptees in the United States today. Behind each of these adoptions are the individual stories and decisions of the parents by birth, parents by adoption, and adopted children. Many people consider adoption one alternative but decide on another. *The Grafted Tree* describes all these individuals and families at the time they make the decision and throughout their lives. It is a practical, "how-to" guide to the legal, administrative and psychological processes of adoption for parents by birth, present and prospective adoptive parents, adopted children, and their families. Decisions about adoption are among the most difficult to make. *The Grafted Tree* is intended to be used as a tool to help make, act on, and live with those difficult decisions.

We, the authors, have first-hand experience with adoption. We are an adoptive father and daughter. Twenty years ago Bill, then Laurie's stepfather, adopted her. As individuals and as a family we've survived various crises, the usual family fights, and still are close and usually enjoy each other's company. Laurie is now grown-up and a social worker. Bill is an attorney and legal writer. We have written this book both as professionals who have counseled and assisted people in making and acting on decisions about adoption, and as an adoptive father and daughter.

What Is Adoption?

Adoption is taking the child of another parent and making him or her your own. It is a legal process and also an emotional process.

Generally, each state sets its own requirements for legal adop-

tion. This can occur in several ways. Often the child's parents by
birth, called the *birthparents, real parents, natural parents,
original,* or *biological parents,* voluntarily give up their rights to
the child. This is called *relinquishment* or *surrender.* Both the
birthmother and the *birthfather* must consent to relinquishment.
Some children are freed for adoption by the death of their parents. Other children are made available for adoption by a court
action, often called an *involuntary termination of parental rights.*
This occurs only when it can be proven in court that a child has
been abandoned or that a parent will probably never be able to
assume parental responsibilities. (The legal process is discussed
in detail in Chapter Four.)

Adoption agencies often arrange adoptions. They can be private charitable institutions, part of county welfare departments,
or state agencies. Usually such agencies free children for adoption
and place children in adoptive homes. Adoptions arranged in this
manner are called *agency adoptions.* (See Chapter Five for a
detailed discussion of agency adoptions.)

In most states adoptions can be arranged by the birthparents
and prospective parents themselves or through the services of an
intermediary, often an attorney or physician. These adoptions are
termed *independent adoptions* or *nonagency adoptions.* A *stepparent adoption,* such as the authors', is a type of independent
adoption in which a stepparent living with a child legally makes
the child his or her own. Requirements for stepparent adoptions
are usually less stringent than for other adoptions. (Chapter Six
describes nonagency adoptions.)

A child and his or her adoptive family are brought together
either through the services of an agency or by independent
means. They live together for several months to a year, depending on the requirements of their state, before the adoption is
finalized. During this time the home usually is investigated and
the family's attorney prepares the legal work for the adoption.
After the mandatory waiting period the family can ask the court to
finalize the adoption. The court will then examine the information
presented and make a decision. (See Chapter Four.) Unless there
is an unusual problem the adoption will be finalized.

Once the adoption is final the *adoptive parents* have the same
legal relationship with the *adoptive child,* or *adoptee,* as parents
have with a *natural child,* a child born to them. The parents are
responsible for the child's well-being, care, and support until
he or she is an adult. In most states the child will have the

same inheritance rights as a natural child. A child's legal ties with his or her birthfamily are erased after adoption. The old birth certificate is removed from the public records, and a new one is issued, giving the child the adoptive parents' name and listing them as parents. The court adoption records and the records of adoption agencies and attorneys are closed. Although the laws vary and are changing, these records are not easily accessible. (See Chapter Eleven.)

Professionals in psychology, psychiatry, and social work often call the emotional process of making a child one's own "becoming a *psychological parent.*" In a legal context this person may be referred to as a *de facto parent.* Psychological parents provide adoptive children with their most important emotional relationship; they are the ones the children trust and look to for care and support. Usually children's birthparents or adoptive parents are also their psychological parents. For some children the psychological parent is another relative or perhaps a *foster parent.* Foster parents are sometimes confused with adoptive parents because they often play such an important and long-term role in a child's life. Foster parents care for children, usually for payment, when the persons responsible for providing care are unable to. Generally foster parents have few or no rights to the children under their care. (The relationship between foster parent and child is further described in Chapter Three.)

How Objective Is this Book?

We have written *The Grafted Tree* to give you a feeling for the people and situations involved in adoption. Concrete information is provided to give you an overview of adoption and to assist you in making and acting on your own decisions. We have tried to be as objective as possible in doing this. However, we do have certain biases.

We think that a sense of family is important for most people, particularly for developing children, who learn to trust and develop a sense of themselves through their early relationships. This need for a family obviously changes as a child becomes older and more his or her own person. Close family relationships come from shared experiences and caring — not from a biological tie. Both birth and adoptive relationships can provide a child and parents with a needed feeling of closeness and belonging.

However, the experience of being a parent or child by adoption is different from the experience of being either by birth. We the authors, don't look at each other and see the same Wishard family nose. Bill never will experience producing and raising a genetically related child and feels a certain amount of loss. Laurie as a young adult needed to search for the heritage of her birthfather. Even now she wonders about the difference adoption has made in her life. Every person has crises and problems, and every relationship has its own strengths, difficulties, and lack of guarantees. This also applies to those of us who are related by adoption. However, we often have some additional and different challenges.

As the authors of this book, we have our own set of professional biases. For Bill, an attorney, qualified legal advice and the protection of individual rights are important. Laurie, a social worker, feels that professional counseling is often helpful and generally favors adoptions through agencies. She believes that the child's best interest should be the first consideration in a decision about adoption.

How to Use "The Grafted Tree"

The Grafted Tree is designed to be a reference and a guide to decision making. The best use can be made of this book not by reading it cover-to-cover but by selecting the parts that are most important to you now. Later, new questions may send you to other parts of the book, or you may want to read the entire book for an overview of the adoption process.

The book is organized chronologically into four parts. Each part contains relevant information for and about birthparents, adoptive parents, and adoptees.

Part I: The Decision introduces the birthparents, adoptive parents, and adoptees at the time of making a decision about adoption. Their options, dilemmas, responsibilities, personal needs, and available resources are discussed, and suggestions are made to assist in making this decision.

Part II: Acting on the Decision describes the procedure by which a child is adopted: the details of how an adoption is arranged, the mechanics of the legal process, and the methods of the adoption agencies and professional people involved. This part also describes and explains intercounty adoptions.

Part III: Creating the New Family Tree discusses the emotional process of adoption for the birthparents, adoptive parents, and adoptee from the time of the adoptee's arrival in his or her new home until adulthood.

Part IV: The Search for the Native Tree introduces adoptees as adults, describes their search for identity and biological roots, and discusses the effects of this search on themselves, their birth-parents, and their adoptive parents. The trend toward an opening of adoption records is also discussed.

The parts are divided into chapters. At the beginning of each chapter you will find an "In General" section, giving you an overview of the chapter. The chapters themselves are broken down into subject areas. Throughout the book examples are given to make the people and situations more real and the material clearer. The first of these follows.

> The Browns have just been told by their doctor that Mr. Brown is unable to father a child. For years they have been planning a family and both Browns are understandably disappointed. Mr. Brown has been quiet and keeping to himself. Mrs. Brown has decided that they should adopt a child. She has talked to her neighbor whose sister adopted a child. Mrs. Brown then called three adoption agencies in town, and went to the bookstore and bought this and three other books on adoption.

Mrs. Brown probably will be unable to restrain herself from reading the entire book cover-to-cover before she falls asleep. However, as she has just begun to think about adoption, she will discover *Part I: The Decision* a good starting point, particularly Chapter Three, The Adoptive Parents. This chapter will suggest to Mrs. Brown that the inability to have a natural child is often a major loss to couples and that it is generally a good idea to get used to this before making a decision about adopting a child.

Later the Browns accept that they are unable to have a natural child but feel they still want children in their lives. They may want to reread the previous chapter and then turn to *Part II: Acting on the Decision*, which will tell them how to find a child, how to deal with adoption agencies, and outline the legal and administrative requirements. Chapter Three, The Child, will also be of interest, since it describes the children available for adoption.

As their decision to adopt becomes firmer they will want to know about the emotional process of adoption, about how to make a child their own, and about the special challenges that come with an adoptive relationship. *Part III: Creating the New Family Tree* and *Part IV: The Search for the Native Tree* will both be helpful with these difficulties.

A Cautionary Note

The Grafted Tree is a general practical guide to adoption. It is not a substitute for the advice of an attorney or for professional counseling. Legal adoptions require the services of an attorney. Professional counseling is recommended as an aid to making decisions about adoption.

To protect the privacy of the individuals and families who have assisted us with this book, the examples presented are not of real people or situations but are composites that reflect general concerns.

Generally we use the term *birthparent* to describe the biological parent of a child. This is our preference. The other terms seem to us more impersonal, uncomfortable, or derogatory. However, *natural parent* is the correct legal term and the term most commonly used by adoption agencies.

ADOPTION
The Grafted Tree

Part I
The Decision

One:

The Birthparents

In General

Fortunate birthparents feel deep joy in learning of pregnancy and the anticipation of raising a child. But many face the news of pregnancy and the reality of being a parent with mixed and scary feelings. For these people there are critical decisions to be made.

They are people in vastly different circumstances. Nancy Green, aged forty-three, married many years with nearly grown children, is now professionally successful and focusing her life on her career. She is unexpectedly pregnant. Sam Rogers, aged nineteen, is a student. The girl he knew only briefly, and does not want to marry, is pregnant. Sam constantly thinks of the child about to be born with feelings of tenderness and caring. A bewildered Mary Randall, aged fifteen, is pregnant and frightened of her parents' anger. And Allison Smith is the mother of a four-year-old she cannot control.

Each of these people faces a very personal decision. They will discover their own needs and abilities, evaluate their choices, and try to make the decision that is best for themselves and their child. Each will be confronted with the reality that there is *no perfect decision.*

This is a difficult period. Most people, though, find making their decision a maturing experience. It is an opportunity to examine the values you may have accepted without question, to take stock of your life, and to discover you have the ability to handle a very difficult problem.

This chapter does not suggest that you, if you are a birthparent, should place your child for adoption. Other choices may be better for you and your child. Described here is the process of making a decision and the *many* choices you have.

(Knowing your legal rights and responsibilities as a parent will help you with your decision. These are discussed in Chapter Four. Refer to Chapter Three for a description of the needs of a child.)

Where to Get Help

Making your decision may be frightening, confusing, and lonely. Many public and private agencies will provide you with information and counseling. Some that may be helpful are:

- Planned Parenthood clinics; these clinics provide pregnancy counseling and are a source of local information and referrals
- a county Welfare Department or Department of Social Services may provide counseling, financial assistance, and referrals
- a community mental health clinic (you do not have to be "crazy" or sick to use their counseling services)
- Family Service Agencies provide counseling
- student counseling centers and student health services
- the Probation or Welfare Department in most communities provides twenty-four-hour-a-day emergency counseling to parents
- Suicide Prevention operates a twenty-four-hour-a-day hotline for anyone needing emergency counseling.

All of these agencies are listed in your telephone directory.

How to Make Your Decision

This decision may seem very different from any you have made before. Well, it probably is. Your responsibility is enormous. Whatever you decide will affect you and your child for a lifetime. Still, making a decision about a pregnancy or an already born child is very much like making any other decision. You will use the same skills in making this decision as you have used to work out other problems in the past.

For most people, making a responsible decision about something important is a process. A decision often involves the following steps:

- discovering you have a problem (you suspect you are pregnant or you are being pressured to place your child for adoption)
- finding out what the problem really is (are you pregnant?)
- developing your choices (what are your options?)
- considering your choices (how will each of your choices affect you and your child?)
- making your decision
- acting on your decision (see Chapters Five and Six if adoption is your decision)

- living with your decision (see Chapters Ten and Eleven if adoption is your decision)

You may be tempted to skip some of these steps. Many who do find they regret it later. You will want to make a responsible decision that is best for you and your child.

Discovering You Have a Problem

Something has changed. You may have missed your last period. Your girlfriend tells you that she is pregnant with your child. Or you have been served with some incomprehensible legal papers telling you that your child is being taken away from you. Whatever the problem, your life is not as simple as it was before.

People react differently to these changes. You probably do not feel your usual self. Some common immediate responses are:

- disbelief
- anger
- confusion
- feeling tired or ill
- embarrassment
- fear
- attempting to ignore the problem

These are very normal feelings. However, these cause you to delay working toward a solution to your problem and may cause you to limit your choices.

Finding Out What the Problem Really Is

The first step in solving a problem is discovering what the problem really is and how much time you have to solve it. Usually, when you are ready to take this step you will begin to feel better and less helpless.

You Suspect You Are Pregnant

Rosanne Francis feels different. She missed her last period, but then she has a new boyfriend, different responsibilities in her job, and she is planning a long-awaited vacation. Maybe it's just the excitement — and it's really very unlikely she could be pregnant.

Rosanne needs to find out whether she is pregnant as soon as possible. A pregnancy test can tell her this as early as ten days after intercourse. She may find out she is not pregnant. Delaying, then, only caused her to worry unnecessarily. Should she find

herself pregnant, early knowledge will give her the choice of a
safe, simple abortion. Waiting too long could eliminate abortion
altogether as an option. If she decides to continue her pregnancy
she will want to protect her own and her baby's health with early
medical care.

Pregnancy tests. Pregnancy is commonly diagnosed in one of
three ways: a blood test, a urine test, and a pelvic examination.
Blood tests are less frequently used, more expensive, but diag-
nose pregnancy ten days after conception. Urine tests are inexpensive, very simple, and usually detect pregnancy six weeks
after the first day of your last period. After you have missed two
periods your doctor, by pelvic examination, can tell if you are
pregnant. No pregnancy test is 100 percent accurate. However, if
your normal periods are regular, if you have missed one period,
and if you have a positive urine test, you can be almost positive
that you are pregnant.

Where to go for a pregnancy test. You may be reluctant to consult
your doctor. If so, other resources are available to you:

- Planned Parenthood birth control clinics
- birth control or abortion clinics listed in the Yellow Pages
  under "Birth Control Information" (try to find a nonprofit
  one)
- local health department
- student health center
- Birthright (Caution — this organization opposes abortion)
- hospital outpatient clinics

Cost. A urine test will cost you from nothing to twenty dollars.
Blood tests cost between fifteen and thirty dollars. As these fees
vary within a given area, you may want to compare prices.

Consent. Many states require minors to have parental consent before having a pregnancy test. Your local Planned Parenthood or
Welfare Department will be able to give you this information.

You Have a Problem Caring for Your Child

> Madeline Grove's two-year-old, Julie, who has not given her
> a moment's peace in the last week, has just broken the TV.
> Madeline finds herself starting to throw little Julie against
> the wall and stops. Madeline knows something is very
> wrong. Maybe she should place Julie for adoption.

Madeline, like many parents, sometimes wonders whether she

should be a parent at all. Other parents may consider adoption after placing their child in foster care and discovering that they do not want the child back.

Whatever your situation, this is the time to get the help of a professional counselor. He or she will help you define the problem and find out how serious it really is. Adoption may not be best for you. For example, you may be experiencing a temporary problem and you may discover that counseling and day-care services will meet your needs and the needs of your child.

Someone Is Trying to Take Your Child Away from You

Your mother may be telling you that if you do not shape up she will adopt your son. You may have received a legal notice informing you of court proceedings to terminate your rights to your child.

Individual situations are different. The laws relating to the rights of parents vary from state to state. *You will want to consult an attorney to find out exactly what your legal situation is.*

For those who cannot afford an attorney, free or inexpensive legal services may be available. You can find them listed in the Yellow Pages under "Community Legal Services" or "Legal Aid." You may have the right to a court-appointed attorney if you are facing legal proceedings.

☑ Caution: Do not delay in responding to a legal notice. Failure to respond may result in your losing your rights to your child.

Developing Your Choices

Your family, friends, or partner may have already decided what they think is best for you. You will want to consider their advice and the realities of your situation. However, do not let them pressure you into a hasty decision or one you do not feel you can live with.

You may discover many options, including the following:

- abortion
- mother raising the child alone (also see Chapters Two and Three)
- father raising the child alone (also see Chapters Two and Three)
- married parents raising the child (also see Chapters Two and Three)
- unmarried parents raising the child together

- the family of one parent cares for the child
- foster care (also see Chapter Three)
- some combination of these choices
- adoption
- doing nothing

You may know already that some of these choices are not right for you. Still, give yourself the freedom to examine each one. You may find that you have overlooked a very useful option.

Abortion

Abortion is the premature termination of a pregnancy. There are four different kinds of abortions:

- spontaneous abortion — usually called a miscarriage
- self-induced abortion — caused by the pregnant woman herself
- criminal abortion — performed by a person other than a licensed physician or under circumstances prohibited by law
- legal abortion — one performed by a licensed doctor following standard medical practices

☑ Warning: Under no circumstances try to induce an abortion yourself or have an abortion performed by anyone other than a licensed physican. These abortions are often unsuccessful and very dangerous to your health.

Since 1973 women have had the right to an abortion during the first six months of pregnancy. This right is only limited by a doctor's willingness to perform the abortion. Generally, during the first fourteen weeks of pregnancy women are able to secure an abortion whatever their reasons.

Early abortions are relatively safe and simple and use one of two medical procedures. In the first, *dilation and curettage (D & C)*, fetal tissue is scraped out of the uterus. In the most widely used method, *suction*, a suction machine removes the contents of the uterus and fetal tissue.

Abortions between sixteen and twenty-four weeks are usually performed by means of *intraamniotic injection*. In this procedure, a fluid is injected through the abdominal wall into the amniotic sac causing the fetus to be expelled — a process very similar to actual labor. Abortions at this stage of pregnancy require that the woman be hospitalized. They are more expensive and carry greater medical risk than earlier abortions.

Later abortions are often upsetting to the woman herself and to hospital staff. A sixteen-week fetus moves and has a distinct heartbeat. A woman twenty weeks pregnant usually feels the fetus move inside her. A fetus born at twenty-four weeks is occasionally able to survive. The level of fetal development and the abortion procedure itself make a late abortion an unpleasant experience and one to be avoided by an early decision.

☑ Note: Under a recent U.S. Supreme Court decision (July, 1979), a minor may obtain an abortion without first securing parental consent to the procedure.

Where to get an abortion. Some local sources of referral for abortions are:

- your own doctor
- Planned Parenthood clinics
- abortion clinics — listed in the Yellow Pages under "Birth Control Information" or "Abortion Clinics"
- student health services

Cost. Abortions during the first fourteen weeks of pregnancy cost between $120 and $200. Later abortions may cost between $500 and $1,000. All abortions cost more if there are medical complications. Private medical plans sometimes pay for abortions. In some states, Medicaid — available through your welfare department — will pay for the abortions of low-income women.

Medical risks. Any medical procedure, including abortion, carries the risk of complications and even death. The medical risks of an early abortion, however, are less than those of a routine tonsillectomy. Many medical authorities state that the medical risks associated with early abortions are less than those associated with childbirth. However, opponents of abortion state that these statistics are biased.

Several studies indicate that women who have had abortions are more likely to experience difficulties with future pregnancies. These studies point to a 15 to 20 percent increase in the likelihood of infertility, premature birth, low birth weight, and abnormal births.

Emotional risks. Many women find abortion the easiest, most convenient way out of an unwanted pregnancy. Abortion will allow you to quickly resume your normal life. Some women find abortion painless — physically and emotionally. Others find themselves regretting an abortion years afterward. Again, early abortions are usually less upsetting.

Abortion rip-offs. Many abortion clinics are profit-making concerns. Some are reported to falsify pregnancy tests in order to
profit from unnecessary abortions. Counseling provided by
profit-making abortion clinics and by those who make referrals to
them is often biased. These clinics stay in business by performing
abortions. Referral sources may receive a referral fee.

Is abortion morally right?

> Rosanne Francis, described earlier, discovers that she really
> is pregnant. She has thought about abortion before — as a
> selfish choice other women might make. Now she thinks of
> herself, and how difficult and changed her life will be when
> she is pregnant.

Deciding about abortion is a real moral and emotional dilemma
for Rosanne. A fetus, whatever its age, is a developing human life.
But her life and her choices are important also. Often there seem
to be compelling and justifiable reasons for abortion. She will
need to sift through all of the conflicting opinions about abortion
and, depending on her own situation and values, decide what is
right for her.

Minimizing risks. The emotional and medical risks associated
with abortion can be minimized. Some of the ways to minimize
risks are:

- early diagnosis of pregnancy — this will allow you
  adequate time to make a thoughtful and early decision
- unbiased professional counseling
- having the abortion performed by a nonprofit clinic or
  your own doctor
- having an abortion within the first fourteen weeks of pregnancy

☑ Reminder: Regardless of your age, you cannot legally be
forced to have an abortion.

Mother Raising the Child Alone

> Chris Olsen is the twenty-seven-year-old unmarried mother
> of a six-month-old son. She decided that marriage with her
> son's father would not work out. Chris, having a good job and
> the support of her family, decided to raise her son herself.
> The boy's father contributes to his support and visits regu-
> larly.

Many women choose to raise a child alone and join the almost
four million American families with children under eighteen

headed by a single parent. While today it is common and more socially acceptable for a single woman to raise her child alone, it is still not easy.

Some women feel that raising a child will give them more independence and make their lives more meaningful. These feelings often fade with the realities of being a single parent. Financially, these women can expect to be disadvantaged. Raising a child is expensive and can limit a woman's earning power. Providing for the emotional and physical needs of a child is at times a strain. And a single woman will be doing this alone.

Since you have choices, consider whether raising a child alone is best for you. Do you want to be a parent? (See Chapter Two, the section, "Do You Want to Be a Parent?") Wanting, though, is not enough. Are you able to provide for a child's needs? Some factors to consider are:

- Are you able to live on your own and handle day-to-day responsibilities like paying the bills and shopping?
- Are you able to tolerate stress and loneliness?
- Do you have family and friends who can help you?
- Do you have a realistic plan to support yourself and your child?
- Do you know how to care for a child physically and emotionally?
- Will you be able to ask for help when you and your child need it?

People, whatever their age, can change their goals and lifestyle. Most of us between the ages of twelve and twenty-five change from children into adults. Raising a child during this period of life can interfere with your own growing up, causing you to miss opportunities and take on responsibilities before you are ready. Your goals will change and your abilities will expand. At fifteen, being a mother may seem your only realistic career. At twenty-five you may consider being an accountant.

Growing up is different for each of us. How mature we are is probably the result of both our physical development and our experiences — not the result of a good or bad character. At eighteen you may be ready to take on the responsibilities of being a parent. Or you may need to wait until you are thirty. Your child, though, will need an adult parent. You do not want to be a child yourself, responsible for raising another child.

A mother who is able to raise her child alone still has a choice. Do you want to raise your child alone? Since you have many responsible alternatives, consider your own needs. Ask yourself:

- Am I finished with my education?
- Will caring for a child cause me to give up a lifestyle that I still want to keep?
- Can I realize my own plans and care for a child too?
- How will caring for a child affect my future relationships?

Any mother, whatever age or marital status, puts aside some of her own desires when she decides to raise a child. Consider what you will be giving up. The benefits of being a parent, raising your child, and having a relationship with your child may far outweigh what you will need to give up. Or they may not. Remember that your happiness is important too. You can make alternative responsible and caring plans for your child.

Father Raising the Child Alone

> Twenty-two-year-old Steve Jones still watches Monday-night football with his friends. But now the group always meets at Steve's apartment. Good babysitters are expensive and hard to find. Steve is the full-time, single parent of his nine-month-old daughter, Kathy.

Increasingly, Steve's choice has become an acceptable one for parents planning for their child. Many fathers happily survive changing diapers, parent-teacher conferences, their child's bout with the measles, and the other day-to-day challenges of being a custodial parent.

A single father raising his child is very much like his female counterpart. He faces many of the same issues in making his decision. Does he want to be a parent? Is he realistically able to care for a child? And, like a female parent, he will need to be a stable adult. (See the previous section, "Mother Raising the Child Alone.")

A father's choices are usually limited. He can suggest but not choose abortion. And often he finds the choice of raising his child by himself available only if the mother does not want to raise the child herself. Then he must show others, generally with more determination and thoroughness than required of a mother, that he is willing and able to be a good parent to his child.

☑ Note: The legal rights of unmarried fathers were expanded by a Supreme Court decision in April, 1978. This is discussed in Chapter Four.

Feelings about fathers having custody and raising their children have changed — but not that much. Many mothers are reluctant to consider or consent to this kind of arrangement. They may have been told that raising a child is a mother's responsibility or that only a very sick or bad mother would allow a child's father to assume this responsibility. However, responsible parents look at all their choices for a child. Then they make a decision according to what is best for them and the child, not according to what people might think of them.

☑ Reminder: Fathers raising their own children should secure a court order giving them custody of their child and specifying the rights and responsibilities of each parent.

Married Parents Raising the Child

> Five years ago Doris and Hugh Mantes married. Doris was then pregnant with the couple's son, David. They had known each other for several years but had postponed marriage until Hugh finished law school. The timing of their marriage was inconvenient for them and a disappointment for their relatives. However, they both felt a strong commitment to their relationship and wanted to be parents eventually.

Marriage is an alternative that solves many of the immediate problems of an unplanned pregnancy or child. By marrying, parents can continue the pregnancy, avoid having an "illegitimate child," raise the child jointly, and themselves have the satisfaction of being married.

Whether you marry or not, both of you will need to decide on a more basic question. Are both of you able and willing to raise your child? After this decision has been made, you can decide whether marriage makes sense for both of you and your child.

Many people marry because they feel marriage is the only responsible choice. Marriage may allow you and your families to feel immediately relieved. However, in the long run marriage may compound your problems. Hasty marriages, particularly between teenagers, fail as often as not. Divorce can be painful and difficult for a couple and their child. The uproar of a divorce sometimes may be harder for a child than being raised by a single parent. Your marriage will be more likely to work out for both of you if:

- even without the child you would want to marry each other
- both of you are good friends as well as lovers

- the responsibilities of marriage and being a parent fit into your current plans

Some married couples find themselves doubting whether they want to raise a child within their marriage or at all. For example, a separating couple may find themselves expecting a child. For them the issue is not deciding whether to marry but deciding if they want to be parents, and then perhaps planning for their child.

☑ Note: Minors may need the consent of their parents or the court or both to marry.

Unmarried Parents Raising the Child Together

Art and Virginia began living together eight months ago. Both are unsure of their commitment to each other and had certainly not planned on becoming parents. When Virginia did become pregnant, neither felt right about terminating her pregnancy. Nor were they ready for marriage or inclined to place the expected child for adoption. They decided to continue their relationship and to become parents.

Many couples who are already living together decide on this alternative. Some feel they can make a commitment to each other and to the child without marriage. Others, like Art and Virginia, both want to raise the child and are not yet certain enough of their relationship to marry.

Whatever your relationship, both of you need to be willing and able to commit yourself to the life-long responsibilities of being a parent. You will each need to be prepared to raise the child alone if your relationship is uncertain. Explore how you would do this. How would you financially support the child? Could both of you agree on where the child would live and how he or she would be educated?

By living together as a family you are acknowledging that the child belongs to both of you. This means that *both* of you will have the legal rights and responsibilities of being a parent until the child is an adult. In many states the father will have equal rights to custody of the child should you separate.

The Family of One Parent Cares for Your Child

Rose, the unmarried mother of newborn Greg, decides that she wants to raise her son herself. She brings Greg to her family home and after several months, it becomes apparent to her and her family that this is not the time for Rose to be a mother. In the meantime Rose's family has become quite attached to young Greg. Greg's aunt, Helen, and her husband take responsibility for Greg. Rose consents to this arrangement.

Your family, perhaps your parents or sister, may be willing and even want to care for or raise your child. Having someone in your family do this has some very obvious advantages. Your child will be able to maintain a relationship with blood relatives, and you probably will be able to keep some type of relationship with your child. Your family *may* be ,able to provide your child with a better home than you can, and you *may* be freed from some parental responsibilities.

Sometimes this arrangement is only temporary. For example, while you complete your final year in college your parents may agree to care for your child. Expect your relative and your child to become close while they are together. In spite of his or her best intentions, your relative may begin to feel like the child's parent and be reluctant to return him or her to your care. The child, too, may prefer to remain in your relative's care.

Be sure that you, your relative, and your child (if old enough to understand) know the reasons for this arrangement. Generally it is best to be definite about the time involved and be specific about each person's responsibilities.

You may consider having your relative take care of the child permanently. The relative will take on all the responsibilities of being a parent and in the child's mind become his or her parent. Is this person the best parent for your child? Does your relative really want to be a parent or is he or she making the offer only to help you out? Is the relative likely to want to and be able to care for your child until he or she grows up?

Many families find this arrangement difficult. Some of the most common problems are:

- The parent later changes his or her mind.
- The children involved are not sure who is responsible for them.
- The parent does not like the way the relative is raising the child.
- The relative disapproves of the parent and limits his or her contact with the child.
- The parent later finds himself or herself physically and financially responsible for the child.

Generally, having a relative raise your child works only if you have confidence in the relative's willingness and ability to be a good "parent" to your child and if you already have a good relationship with this relative.

Often this is the best choice for the parent of an older child. Attachments have probably developed between the child and other members of the family. The relative may already be your child's "parent." This choice may provide your child with a stable parental relationship, prevent the loss of family ties, and allow you to maintain some kind of relationship with your child. (See Chapter Three, the section, "Older Children.")

Be sure to provide yourself and your child with legal safeguards if you choose this alternative. Relatives move, fight, and change. Your child will need the security of knowing that he or she will be raised until adulthood by the same person. You will need to know what your rights and responsibilities are. Discuss with an attorney whether guardianship or adoption would be appropriate in your situation. (For further discussion, refer to Chapter Four, The Legal Process, and Chapter Six, the section, "Family Adoptions.")

Foster Care

Foster care is a temporary arrangement in which someone other than the child's parent or relative provides twenty-four-hour care. Usually the foster parent is paid for this service. Arrangements for voluntary foster care can often be made through your local welfare department or Department of Social Services, or a private children's agency. An agency representative, generally a social worker, supervises the placement. Financial assistance is often available.

Sometimes foster care is involuntary. This occurs when a child is placed by court order and this is usually the result of the child's parents or guardian being neglectful, abusive, or unwilling or unable to care for the child. The child will return to the parent or guardian only when the original problem has been corrected and with court orders.

Placing your child in foster care gives you *time*. You may need this time in order to become the kind of parent you want to be. This might mean finishing vocational training or continuing intensive counseling. Or you may need time to decide on a plan for your child. Parents often place their children in foster care while they make a decision about adoption.

> Twenty-year-old Anna is a single woman who has just given birth to a daughter. At this point Anna and the baby's father are uncertain whether to raise the child themselves or place her for adoption.

The social worker supervising the foster placement of Anna's child helped her plan for herself and her daughter. Together they developed a plan, which like many case plans was in writing, and included:

- the reasons for the foster placement
- the expected time of the placement
- what the parent will be doing to change her situation
- what the social worker will be doing to help the parent
- the arrangements and frequency of the parents' visits to the child
- how the parent and the agency will handle any problems and changes in plans

Foster care can be helpful to parents and children only if it is temporary. Sometimes parents place their children in foster homes for months and find the months drifting into years. Long-term foster care can leave children in limbo, unsure whether they belong to their birthparents or to their foster parents. *Plan on one year as the maximum acceptable time for your child to remain in foster care.* Consider another choice if the plan requires more time. (See Chapter Three for a discussion of the emotional impact of foster care on a child.)

☑ Warning: Parents who allow their children to remain in foster care for a long period of time lose contact with their children; those who do not follow through on their agreements with the supervising agency can lose their rights to their child.

Some Combination of these Choices

Often a combination of several alternatives can make the best plan. For example, a high-school parent is unlikely to have the maturity of the financial resources to raise a child alone. Often until the parent is an adult a grandparent will raise the child. Some parents choose to raise their child alone until they are in a better position to marry the other parent.

The major difficulty of this type of plan is that it often involves many changes in the child's home and caretaker. Frequent disruptions can prevent a child from feeling secure and wanted. (See Chapter Three.)

Adoption

For parents who wish to continue with the pregnancy or who already have a child, adoption may be the alternative of choice. By placing your child for adoption you will no longer be responsible for his or her physical and emotional care, financial support, and planning. You will be free to continue your normal life without the restrictions of a child. You lose, of course, all legal rights and ties to your child.

You may not want to be a parent now, or perhaps ever, if you know that the responsibilities of being a parent will make your life miserable. Listen to yourself. Trapped, unwilling parents, in spite of their best intentions, communicate their feelings to their children. Accepting the role of a parent under these circumstances will make both you and your child unhappy. You can still be responsible and caring by planning for your child, even by letting him or her go.

Most birthparents find that their feelings are very mixed. They realize their situation is not ideal for raising a child, and they are reluctant but able to make the changes in their lives needed to raise a child. Their most important concern is whether adoption would be best for their child.

Some of the possible benefits your child may find in adoption are:

- a two-parent family
- financial security
- educational opportunities
- adult, stable parents
- the opportunity for a traditional family life
- parents who choose to be parents

Of course, adoption does not guarantee any of these. Adoptive parents divorce, go bankrupt, and get sick like other parents.

But the risks can be minimized, particularly if your child is white, under two years old, and healthy. Work with a reputable adoption agency. Your child's welfare will be their first consideration. They will exhaustively screen prospective adoptive parents and try to match your child with the best parents possible. They will consider your preferences and may even let you help choose the adoptive parents. (See Chapter Five, Agency Adoptions.)

You can also minimize the risks by placing your child for adoption as early as possible. Young children are more sought after for adoption. If your child is young, you and the agency can be more selective in your choice of adoptive parents. Additionally, a young child is less likely to be affected by the experiences before his or her adoption and adjusts more easily to a new family.

Aside from the lack of total certainty about the success of your child's adoptive placement, there are other possible problems to be considered:

- Adopted children do not have a biological tie to their adoptive families.
- Adopted children wonder about their birthfamilies and why they were placed for adoption.
- As adults children may attempt to reestablish contact with their birthparents.
- You probably will feel a great sense of loss when you place your child for adoption.
- You may always miss your child and wonder how he or she is doing.

Of all the choices, adoption is often the most difficult to accept. It is a permanent and usually voluntary severing of one of life's most important relationships — the relationship between parent and child.

Usually parents choose to place their child for adoption because they care very much for the child. They have considered more than their own wishes. They have evaluated their own needs and the needs of their child. They may decide that adoption, even with its uncertainties, will give their child more than they can. Coming to this decision requires the strength to handle personal loss and the maturity to see beyond their own needs.

(The choice of adoption is discussed throughout this book. However, Chapter Three describes in detail a child's own needs, the availability of adoptive families, and the immediate effects of adoption on a child. Chapters Four, Five and Six describe the practical and legal aspects of arranging an adoption.)

Doing Nothing

> Susan Howe is eight months pregnant. She has yet to see a doctor or make any plans for the coming child. While her parents, friends, and boyfriend prod, yell, sympathize, and threaten, Susan watches TV.

Even by doing nothing you cannot avoid making a decision. *You are deciding not to decide.* Eventually someone will decide for you. The court may remove your child from your care or one of your relatives may simply begin caring for him or her.

By not committing yourself to any plan, both you and your child lose. You lose the satisfaction of confronting a difficult problem and doing the best you can. You allow yourself to become helpless and powerless. And you will probably feel guilty for the damage your inaction causes your child.

Your child may lose even more. He or she may never experience having a stable, committed, loving parent.

Considering Your Choices

> Last year Rosanne Francis, nineteen, graduated from high school and began working in a print shop. She is still living with her parents and thinks of getting an apartment of her own someday and maybe continuing her education. She met Jim Connor, twenty, four months ago. Jim is a junior college student, works part-time, and plans a career as a police officer. Until now neither Rosanne nor Jim has thought seriously about the permanence of their relationship or their commitment to each other. Rosanne is two months pregnant.

Rosanne has recovered from the shock of discovering that she is pregnant and is aware that she does have choices. She is also aware that time is a factor. If she wants an abortion she should decide within the next six weeks. None of her choices seem acceptable to her. Rosanne, like other birthparents, discovers that she will need to compromise.

This is a complex decision, not totally dependent on the wishes, values, or abilities of the birthparents. Like Rosanne, consider each choice in the light of:

- your own needs, values, and abilities
- what a child needs (see Chapter Three)
- what the other parent, your family, and your friends can offer
- what outside resources are available to you

Rosanne asked Jim and her family what their thoughts were. Her family offered to help her financially with the costs of an abortion or childbirth, but they did not feel they could help with raising a child. Jim did not feel he was ready for marriage or raising the child himself. He thought either abortion or adoption were the best choices. Rosanne was now able to rule out many of the choices as impractical.

She then began the hard work of looking at herself and the way her life was going. How did she really feel about abortion? Did she really want to go back to school? Why did she let herself get pregnant? Did she want to become a parent? Like many people, she found making a decision a real incentive to become aware of how she was choosing to live her life.

This is a decision that is different for everyone. Consider the advantages and disadvantages of each choice for you and your child. What problems will each present? What rewards?

Making Your Decision

You may feel very lonely while making your decision. And you are. No one can understand exactly how you feel or totally appreciate your dilemma. But it may be helpful to confide in someone. You may need someone to help you get a perspective on the situation. There are resources to help you with your decision and to give you support.

Family and Friends

Many people find that after their family and friends get over the initial shock they are very helpful. Often this is a time when families actually become closer.

Not everyone will be able to give you what you need. Some will already have a definite opinion about what you should do and may try to pressure you into a particular choice. Think about your choices carefully before you confront your family and friends. But do listen to them. They know you and they may have some constructive suggestions.

Who should you tell? You will definitely need to tell your child's other parent if you are considering any choice other than abortion. The decision will be his also. Depending on your relationship, he may be a valuable source of insight and financial and emotional support.

Your own family, perhaps your parents or your sister, may be very supportive to you. Or they may be so disturbed by what is happening to you that they are unable to get beyond their own feelings. Your situation will require them to adjust and to change also. Your father, for example, may finally need to realize that you are no longer a child. Give your family some time. They may surprise you with their ability to respond to your needs.

You will need the help of your family if you are still in high school and plan to finish your education. They will be your primary financial resource. If you decide to raise the child yourself they will be essential to your plan.

Counseling

Counseling will not tell you what to do. It may help you clarify your feelings and get a perspective on your situation. Counselors are human and may have their own feelings about what would be best for you. A good counselor may make suggestions but will not decide for you. Your counselor can help you understand why you are confused — your feelings and your conflict — and help you evaluate your choices and learn from your experience. You may want to involve your family or your child's other parent in counseling.

The counseling agencies that may be located in your community are listed at the beginning of the chapter.

Specific Services

A variety of specific services may be available in your community. These services can help you while you are making your decision and offer you the resources to act on your decision.

AFDC (Aid to Families with Dependent Children) and Medicaid. AFDC offers direct financial assistance and is usually called welfare. This minimal payment is available to needy families. Medicaid provides assistance with medical costs, sometimes including the cost of an abortion. This assistance is available through your welfare department.

Maternity Homes. Maternity homes provide twenty-four-hour residential care for pregnant women. Usually food, shelter, counseling, and medical care are available. In the past, maternity homes were places for pregnant girls to hide until they placed their children for adoption. Recently their role has expanded considerably. Most will help you whatever your plan is for your child. A maternity home can be a valuable resource for a woman whose family is in uproar because of her pregnancy. It can also be a place where you can make a decision. Some maternity homes can be a valuable resource for a woman whose family is in uproar because of her pregnancy. It can also be a place where you can make a decision. Occasionally, maternity homes will provide a sheltered living situation for young women and their children.

Miscellaneous Services. Your community may provide special educational programs, vocational training, and child-care services for young, single, or low-income parents. Check with your Department of Education and your welfare department for the availability of these services.

Involuntary Termination of Parental Rights

> Susan Howe, mentioned earlier, never did make a decision about her child. After Karen, her daughter, was born, she was placed in a temporary foster home. Susan was given time to make plans. A year later Susan is still watching television and still has done nothing. The county welfare department wants to place Karen for adoption and is attempting to terminate Susan's parental rights.

In these legal proceedings a parent's rights to a child can be ended without his or her consent. Generally agencies and courts will not initiate these proceedings unless they have good cause. First, it is extremely difficult to terminate parental rights. Second, an agency generally does not wish to assume responsibility for additional children. (See Chapter Four for a more in-depth explanation of the legal proceedings.)

You can be sure something is very wrong if your situation has deteriorated to this point. Your child is missing something important in his or her life. Perhaps your child has been in a foster home for years and you are unlikely to care for him or her again. Or maybe a chronic illness permanently prevents you from caring for your child.

It will not help your child to let your pride or anger at the agency get in the way of doing what is best for the child. Find out what the agency or court plans for your child. Can you offer the child something better? If you cannot, you may want to give the agency permission to go ahead with their plan. This will avoid costly and painful court proceedings.

An agency wants what is best for your child. Show them a plan that is as good or better than their own and they may cooperate with you. Some alternate plans are:

- arranging for your child to be adopted
- allowing a friend, relative, or foster parent to become your child's guardian (transferring legal custody to that person)
- radically changing the way you live

Making the Decision and Acting upon It

You will reach a point, perhaps as a result of a deadline you have set for yourself, when you know it is time to make your decision. You will have sorted out your feelings and considered the choices. Still, you are not certain. Do not expect yourself to be free of doubts. *You cannot make a perfect decision – only the best possible decision at this time.*

Before you commit yourself to your decision ask yourself one last time:

- Is this my own decision or what someone else wants me to do?
- Have I considered all the choices?
- Will this choice meet my child's basic needs?

Once you have made your decision you will want to act on it. (See Part II.) Your decision may not be final, and perhaps you will need to back up and consider your choices again if you find yourself delaying.

Living with Your Decision

Whatever you have decided, the process of making this decision has probably changed you. You have learned about yourself. You have a more definite idea of who you are rather than who you should be. You are probably surer of your goals. Your family may consider you differently. You know you have the ability to handle a difficult problem and reach a decision. (Chapters Ten and Eleven describe the experiences of birthparents and parents after adoption.)

Handling Feelings of Loss

Expect to feel some immediate loss or grief. You have given up something, whether it be a pregnancy, a child, or the freedom from parental responsibilities. A feeling of loss or grief is a normal reaction and should become less acute as time goes by. Some people find themselves unable to get on with their normal lives. You may want to involve yourself in professional counseling if this happens to you.

How Will You Feel Later about the Decision?

Usually people feel better about the decision when they have not taken short cuts in making it. Years later they look back, remembering that they thoughtfully considered their alternatives, confronted their values and realities, and made the best choice available to them. People who are not pressured into their decision and who are assisted by counseling generally are most satisfied with their decisions.

Two:

The Adoptive Parents

In General

Most of us grew up believing that someday we too would become parents. We also believed in storks. As adults we find that the expected does not always happen. Some of us decided not to become parents. Some of us became parents and wish we had not. Others of us are never able to have the child we want. As adults we learn to handle the realities of our own needs and disappointments.

We also find that we have choices about the kinds of lives we want to live. Many people consider adopting a child only when they feel their choice has been taken away. But prospective adoptive parents are people who *have* choices. This chapter describes the choices that may be available to you and offers you some guidelines for making a decision about adoption.

You, like most people thinking about adoption, have probably thought about the risks, uncertainties, and responsibilities of adopting a child. Already you realize what a difficult decision this is. Adoptive parents do not just drift into becoming parents. They knowingly and thoughtfully choose. You will gather information; talk to people; examine yourself, your lifestyle, and your relationships; and finally make your decision.

Considering Your Choices

For every decision there must be at least two choices. You will have more than that. Allow yourself to consider all of them. Each is a respectable choice. Although you may discover others here are some of your possible choices:

- not to become a parent
- for some, not to become the parent of another child
- to postpone your decision about adopting a child
- for some, to have a birthchild

- to adopt a child
- to find some other way to have children in your life, such as becoming a day-care or foster parent

Consider each of these options. How would each affect your life? What are the problems of each? What would each give to you? Making a decision about a child is first and foremost an individual decision. Regardless of what your family wants, *you* will be committing yourself to a relationship. Do not let yourself be pressured into a family decision that is not right for you.

Then you and your partner and perhaps your children will want to discuss the choices. You may find that other family members feel very differently about the choices. They are neither right nor wrong. They simply feel one way or another. Being honest with each other is crucial at this point. You do not want to discover when your son is a teenager that your wife never wanted a child. Some of the differences may not be important, but now is not the time to adopt a child if either you or your spouse has any major doubts or differences.

Do You Want to Be a Parent?

Making the decision to adopt a child really means making two decisions. First you need to decide whether you want to be a parent at all. Later you can decide if you want to be an adoptive parent. The couple described below are beginning to make these decisions.

> Sue and Bob King are in their late twenties. When they married seven years ago, they planned that in several years Sue would become pregnant, leave her job, and begin the work of raising a family. Sue is reluctantly still at the same job. For some unknown reason she never became pregnant, and she has now given up on ever having a birthchild. She is still anxious to begin her real career — being a parent. Bob seldom thinks anymore about having a child, but he believes Sue would be a lot happier with a child. His own parents keep asking him when he and Sue will finally start a family. Sue has suggested recently that they could adopt a child.

Like most prospective adoptive parents, the Kings are learning a lot about themselves in the process of making a decision. Bob now wonders if he wants to be a parent at all, and Sue has doubts about being an adoptive parent. Both are hesitant and have difficulty even talking between themselves about adoption.

As a starting point the Kings could consider if any of the following statements describe their feelings:

- I will be miserable without a child.
- I want a child more than my husband or wife.
- I want a child because it is expected of me.
- I want a child to be my companion.
- My job, education, or interests leave me little time for a child.

Any of the above statements, if true, are good indications that now is *not* the time to become a parent. The Kings have a choice. People are responsible for their own happiness. A child can add to your life but cannot compensate for your feelings of unhappiness or incompleteness as a person. In fact, children seldom help marriages or make unhappy people happy. Even if they could, it is unfair to place such a responsibility on them. Children need parents who are healthy, stable, mature adults and who can provide for their child's physical, emotional, and financial needs.

The Kings realized that now was not the time to make a decision about a child. They found that they were both unhappy and unsure even about their marriage. People do change, however. Their marriage survived, and several years later these two much happier people decided to become parents.

People want to be parents for a variety of reasons — most of them selfish. But being a parent should meet your own needs as well as those of the child. Most of us are complicated people, and our feelings and motives are usually mixed. You may want to become a parent because you enjoy children and want the experience of raising a family. You may want to be part of a child's growth, sharing in his or her accomplishments and joys. Or, you may want to have grown children when you are older and the experience of being a grandparent. In most cases, fortunately, your needs will coincide with a child's.

Should You Choose Not to Be an Adoptive Parent

Being an adoptive parent is not exactly the same as being a parent by birth. Many people who want to be parents choose not to become adoptive parents. These are not unloving, snobbish, or bigoted people. They are simply people who for a variety of reasons have decided that adoption will not meet their own or a child's needs.

Some reasons *not* to adopt a child are:

- You do not feel an adoptive child could ever be your own.
- You feel that adopting a child is settling for second best.
- You would not be able to confide in your friends, family, or an adopted child about the adoption.
- You are afraid that the child would make the same mistakes or have the same problems as his or her birthparents.
- You feel that adopting a needy child is your religious, moral, or political duty.
- You could not accept a child whose abilities were very different from your own.

The decision not to adopt a child is as difficult to make as the decision to adopt. Still, in this time of choices, your family and friends may tell you that you ought to become some type of parent. *Listen to yourself.*

Challenges for Adoptive Parents

No child comes with a guarantee. Your bundle of joy may grow up to be a sleazy, dope-smoking motorcycle fiend. Birth and adoptive parents are routinely surprised and disappointed as well as delighted by their offspring. Adoptive parents have the usual trials and joys that come with being a parent, along with some additional challenges. (See Chapters Nine and Eleven.)

Adopted children and their biological heritage. Your adopted child will not inherit his or her appearance or abilities from you. You may be a person who struggles to write a "thank you" note and find yourself the parent of a child with a talent for writing. Nevertheless, your influence and encouragements will be crucial to your child whatever his or her talents. Like all parents, you may be disappointed. Perhaps you had always wanted to share your love for sports with your child, but your son has the ability to connect with air not a tennis ball. Adoptive parents need more than the usual degree of flexibility and acceptance of a child's individuality.

Accepting your inability to have a birthchild. Many people considering adoption are unable to have a birthchild. For most people this inability is a major personal loss. Since we have been raised to think of our fertility as a central part of our identity as adult men and women, most people experience shock, anger, a sence of failure, and depression when they find that they cannot have a birthchild. Eventually they accept this, as they have other disappointments, and realize that the ability to give birth has little to do with their value as adults or parents.

Do *not* immediately try to replace the birthchild you will never have with an adopted child. Your sense of worth will return. Then you can decide to adopt, when you feel good about yourself and your ability to be a parent. People who never adjust to the fact of their infertility often see adoption as a failure and their adopted child as a second choice. Later they may be unable to discuss the adoption with either their child or their family.

Accepting your child's background. You and your child's birthparents are allies, not competitors. Both of you want the best for your child. Children need to know that they were adopted, why they were adopted, and something about their birthparents. This information will come from you.

Children may feel rejected when they understand what adoption means. "What was wrong with me that made my 'real' mother not want me?" Adopted children feel better about themselves if they believe that their birthparents cared for them. They need to know that their birthparents made a responsible, loving decision in placing them for adoption, when this is true.

Children will wonder if they are like their birthparents. Children often believe they can inherit their birthparents' mistakes and traits as well as the color of their eyes. Your child's birthparents may have had very serious difficulties. An adopted child may ask, for example, "Since my mother was in jail, will I go there too?" You will need to be sensitive and honest in discussing such questions. Children should not feel that their birthparents were villains, or that they will repeat their mistakes.

You can present your child's background to him or her in a positive way if you feel positively about it yourself. Many people can understand and sympathize, for example, with the dilemma of an unmarried birthparent. However the same people may find it difficult to understand a birthparent who abused or molested a child. Do not adopt a child whose background or birthparents are totally repugnant to you.

Handling outsiders and outside help. From the beginning, adoptive parents find themselves losing their privacy. They are investigated to determine their suitability as adoptive parents. Very personal questions are asked. Their home is visited. Their doctor, friends, and employers will be asked for references. The child's placement will be supervised from the time he or she enters their home until the adoption is final.

Acquaintances, friends, and family will be curious. They will ask you about the child and why you decided to adopt. Be prepared for insensitive questions, such as, "Why couldn't you have your own child?" and "Don't you worry that he'll turn out like his real mother?" You will find yourself interesting to others, most people will have an opinion about what you are doing.

Sometimes the help of outsiders will be welcome. Adoptive parents need to have faith in their own abilities and the sense to know when a problem is beyond their resources. You will particularly want help when adopting an older or handicapped child.

Helping your child handle being adopted. Your child will have an extra task growing up. As a parent you will give your child love, security, and a family. But adopted children will still need to understand why they were adopted, accept this, and realize that both their birth and adoptive backgrounds are part of their identity. They may wonder about their birthfamilies, frequently doubt if they belong, and often feel different. This does not happen because you have failed as parents or because your child does not love you. It is simply part of the process of growing up. You are the ones he or she has trusted in the past. You will be the ones he or she will want to turn to for help and support with this problem.

Do You Want to Be an Adoptive Parent?

You want to be a parent, but you still have some doubts about adoption. You have thought about what adoption will mean to you. You are reasonably sure that you will be a good parent and can meet the challenges of being an adoptive parent — but not totally sure. *Most people are not.* In every adoption, as in every relationship, there is an element of risk.

Naturally you will want to eliminate as many of these doubts as possible before you decide to adopt. Ask yourself these questions:

- Could I accept a child with interests and abilities very different from my own?
- Am I willing to accept outside help?
- Will I be able to talk to others and to my child about the adoption?
- For me, is adopting a child a first choice rather than second best?

- Can I deal with information about an adopted child's past?
- Does my husband or wife also want to adopt a child (if applicable)?

Answering yes to all of these questions should eliminate some of your natural uncertainties.

In the end you will have to ask yourself the most important question of all: Do I and my family want to make a life-long commitment to a child? This decision is your own.

Help in Making the Decision

Deciding whether to adopt is not easy. Most people take time, gather information, and talk to others. They sort out what they have learned about adoption and themselves and then make their decision. There are resources to help you with your decision.

Adoption Agencies

Adoption agencies will give you information about the emotional and legal processes of adoption. Usually they will provide you with counseling to help you come to a decision. If they feel that you want to adopt for the wrong reasons, they will tell you and they will not place a child with you.

Adoptive Parents' Associations and Other Adoptive Parents

Usually a local adoption agency will be able to refer you to a local or regional adoptive parents' association. This type of group is often social and is composed of adoptive parents and their families. Adoptive parents' groups, and adoptive parents in general, are generally very willing to give you a first-hand view of what being an adoptive parent is really like.

Experience with Children

Many people think about becoming parents but have never actually cared for children on a full-time basis. Your nephew Tommy can be a delight when you take him to the ball game for an afternoon. He changes into a total rascal when you try to get him to school on time. Spend a weekend, or better yet a week, caring for a child. This will give you a chance to find out if you really enjoy children and help you form a realistic idea of what a child in your life will mean.

Who Adopts?

> Roberta and Jim Eden are a couple in their early thirties. Roberta works as a bookkeeper and Jim is a teacher. Although their income is only moderate, both of them enjoy their jobs. They have always been busy people. Jim is an amateur actor, and Roberta has accepted private bookkeeping clients. They often spend time with Jim's family, who live nearby. Three years ago they decided they wanted to have children and found that Roberta was unable to conceive a child. Both were very disappointed. They still wanted to become parents and decided to adopt a child. Several months ago they adopted three-year-old Debbie.

There is no standard or ideal adoptive parent. Parents, like children, are individuals. But adoption agencies (most people adopt through agencies) usually have some general requirements. They want parents to be happy, stable, well functioning adults. Such agencies usually prefer a couple who has been married at least three years. They want people who are flexible in their expectations and can tolerate stress.

Parents are expected to have problems. Life is full of disappointments and conflicting needs. Adoption professionals look at how people live with disappointments and work out their differences.

Adoption professionals also look closely at what the prospective adoptive parents can give to a child. This will vary with the needs of each specific child. In general, the bottom line is that the adoptive parents must be able to provide the child with basic financial, emotional, and physical security, and as well as with acceptance and love.

Specific Concerns

Adoption professionals usually try to be conservative when placing a child. They do take risks, but only when they feel it is in the best interests of the child to do so. *As prospective adoptive parents you do not have the right to a child.* You can expect to be treated courteously, fairly, and to have your questions answered. You cannot expect to be given a child.

Chapter Five discusses adoption agencies — how they operate, their staff, and what to do if you believe that you are being treated unfairly. Refer to Chapter Four for a description of the specific legal requirements for adoptive parents.

Professionals consider their first priority to be the child's right to the best placement possible. Often a child has been relinquished by birthparents who want their child to have a more traditional type of family life than they are able to provide. Agencies try to respect such wishes.

Some would-be adoptive parents find the requirements of agencies too traditional and rigid. If an agency rejects you, consider their reasons carefully. Often the reason is valid, and you would probably have problems if you adopted a child.

Not all agencies have the same requirements. Another agency's requirements might not bar you from adoption, or you might want to consider an independent, or nonagency, adoption as a way to avoid the requirements.

Availability of Children

In general, the more flexible you are in your choice of children, the greater your chances of being able to adopt. Older and hard-to-place children are readily available to qualified parents. However, if you want a healthy, white, newborn child you should expect to wait one to five years. In fact, you may never be able to adopt such a child. (See Chapter Three.)

Age

Adoptive parents must be adults. However, while you may be of legal age, expect an adoption agency to be skeptical about placing a child with you if you are under twenty-five.

Adoption agencies seldom place an infant with parents over forty, since the parents would be in their mid-fifties when the child is a teenager. But agencies do place older and hard-to-place children with older parents. (See Chapter Three.)

Marital Status

Adoption agencies usually prefer to place children with married couples. Some professionals believe children need the close relationships with adults of both sexes and the model for intimacy that a married couple provides. Parenting any child is a difficult task alone. A single adoptive parent will need to provide a child with the company of adults of both sexes. As a parent, he or she will need the support of family and friends. Nevertheless, the trend is toward more single-parent adoptions. Single adults, however, can usually only expect to adopt older or hard-to-place children. (See Chapter Three.)

Divorce

Some agencies consider a divorce a barrier to adoption. Most agencies will want to know the reasons for the divorce and will be concerned about the length and stability of your current marriage. Adoption professionals realize that everyone changes, makes mistakes, and has problems. They will be most concerned about how the divorce affects your current relationship and your ability to be a parent.

Financial Means

You do not need to be wealthy to adopt a child. However, you should not have an intimate relationship with your bill collector. A family that is always unsure how they are going to meet their normal expenses does not need another child.

Often families with low or moderate incomes provide excellent homes for children. To encourage low-income families to adopt, some agencies will waive their fees, as well as arranging to have legal costs paid. Some states facilitate the adoption of hard-to-place children by offering low-income families adoption subsidies. (See Chapter Three for a description of children who are eligible to receive adoption subsidies, and Chapter Five, the section, "Adoption Subsidies."

Parents Working outside the Home

Some, but not all, adoption agencies expect one parent — usually the mother — to remain home with the child until the adoption is final. Realistically, the introduction of a child into a home requires adjustment on everyone's part. Whether you are employed outside your home or not, you will need to spend much of your time with a newly adopted child. Many employers give adoption leaves.

Parents Who Can Have Birthchildren

Professionals frequently feel that people who cannot have birthchildren deserve first priority in adoptions. As a result, the ability to have children is often a barrier to adoption. Increasingly, though, even fertile people are choosing to have their children or complete their families by adoption rather than by birth. Often they feel that the world already has enough children or that they would not like to be the parent of an infant.

Adoption professionals will also be concerned with prospective adoptive parents' reasons for choosing not to have a birthchild. They may be suspected of being afraid of childbirth or perhaps of being subtly rejecting.

Health

Prospective adoptive parents should be physically healthy. A parents' uncertain or failing health is frightening to the parent as well as to his or her family. This is not a preferred environment for anyone, especially a child. While no one, of course, can be certain of his or her continued health or survival, children need parents who can expect to be alive and in good health until the children are adults.

Some chronic, manageable medical conditions, such as certain types of diabetes, are not a barrier to adoption. In fact, for a diabetic child learning to manage his own condition, a diabetic adoptive parent may be preferred.

Race and Religion

Professionals try to match the race and religion of a child's adoptive parents with the race and religion of a child's birthparents. You may find that an adoption agency does not have a child who will match with you.

Some agencies require that you be a member in good standing of a religious group. Most agencies will be concerned if a married couple is of two very different religions. They will want to know if this is a problem in your marriage and how it may affect the way you raise a child.

Past Problems

Everyone has a skeleton in their closet. We grow up experimenting, sometimes making mistakes, and learning from them. Would-be adoptive parents are often fearful, with good reason, that a past problem such as psychiatric hospitalization, a criminal conviction, drug use, or an illegitimate pregnancy will make it impossible for them to adopt a child.

What will be most important to an agency, and even more important to you, is how this affects your functioning and your ability to be a parent *now*. How long ago did you have this problem? Why did it occur? What did you learn from it? How would you react to the stress of a child? How do you feel about yourself now?

Unusual Lifestyles

This term is used to cover a variety of very different and individual situations. You may be an unmarried couple, live in a commune, or be a homosexual. Remember you do not have the right to a child. However, there may be a child who *needs* the special type of home you can provide.

Working with an agency will be difficult. They probably will be skeptical of what you can offer a child. But work with them. You and the agency have the same goal — the best for the child. A child deserves the best parents possible. Convince an agency that you will be a good parent, and you will become more confident of this yourself.

Three:
The Child

In General

A child is an individual, growing and constantly learning. Children are born with a biological heritage and potential that are affected by experience throughout their lives. The children available for adoption are no different. This chapter describes these children, their background, their potential, their availability for adoption, and their needs — as related both to normal growth and to their adjustment to adoption.

Children stubbornly resist categorization, labels, and generalities. Writers, professionals, policy makers, and adults in general, however, appear to live by them. In general, there seem to be two varieties of children available for adoption — the wanted and the less wanted. Governmental and agency policies on adoption differ, depending on which group a child falls into.

The children in the first group — healthy, normal, white children under two years of age — are the least available and most sought after for adoption. As a result adoption agencies and birthparents can be extremely selective in their choice of adoptive parents for this group. As mentioned earlier, prospective adoptive parents wanting white, healthy babies should be prepared to wait.

But this situation may be changing. Some adoption agencies indicate that the increase of pregnancies among very young women (under sixteen) has made many more white infants available for adoption. However, this may be only a temporary and regional change.

The second group contains the "hard-to-place" children — older children, groups of brothers and sisters, children with medical, emotional, or educational problems, and children with minority or mixed racial backgrounds. Adoption agencies actively recruit families for these children. If money is a barrier to adoption, adoption subsidies can often be arranged. No licensed adoption agency or responsible professional will make an adoptive placement they consider inappropriate for either parents or child. However, agencies are inclined to act on applications more quickly, be more flexible in their requirements, and take greater risks, when seeking homes for hard-to-place children. Would-be adoptive parents who are single, over forty, already have several children, or have unconventional lifestyles probably will only be able to adopt hard-to-place children. Birthparents wanting to relinquish hard-to-place children should ask their adoption agency for information on the availability of adoptive homes.

What Do Children Need As They Grow Up?

No one, including the authors, has satisfactorily answered this question, which is debated constantly by scientists, professionals, parents, and children. However, there is general agreement on certain basic notions of child development and children's needs, some of which follow:

- At birth children are totally dependent on others for care. This need diminishes as they get older.
- Even newborn children are aware of their surroundings. As they grow they become increasingly aware of and affected by people, places, feelings, and changes.
- Children change very rapidly during their first six years. Not only do they grow physically but their methods of communicating, their patterns of thinking, and their needs also change.
- Children are continually learning. How they react to new experiences depends on what they have learned in the past.
- Children need to form a strong attachment with a reliable and caring adult. From this relationship they learn how to form other relationships.

For children who are to be adopted this means:

- The earlier they can begin forming permanent parental relationships the better.
- And the fewer changes in parents, caretakers, or homes the better.

The Infant and the Young Child

David, like most two-month-old babies, smiles when he recognizes familar people, and he is beginning to develop his own personality. He is very active, he is a greedy eater, and he demands attention, whether gained by his charming smile or by a scream. His parents, Jenny and Chris, are unmarried high school students, both seventeen and still living with their own parents. When she was six months pregnant with David, Jenny was helped by her parents to go to an adoption agency for counseling. Both young parents met with an agency counselor many times before deciding to place David for adoption. After he was born, David was placed in a temporary foster home. Jenny and Chris visited their son and then formally relinquished him to the agency for adoption. The agency has monitored David's development closely and is convinced that he is a healthy, normal infant. He is now ready for placement with an adoptive family.

The Waiting Period

Infants like David who are placed through agencies usually stay several weeks to several months in a foster home before they are placed with adoptive families. The professionals working with David realize that he will have grown and made attachments before he is placed in an adoptive home. But they delay his placement for several reasons. His birthparents need to be sure of their decision. Agencies usually wait at least a week after a child's birth before permitting the parents to relinquish the child. This gives the parents time to recover from the birth, reflect on their decision, and make their goodbyes to the child. Sometimes the agency must go to court to free a child for adoption, and this further delays his or her placement. (See Chapter Four, The Legal Process.)

The agency also wants to be sure that the baby is healthy. By means of thorough medical examinations, the observations of temporary foster parents, and a complete medical history of the birthparents, an agency is usually reasonably certain of a child's health when he or she is between three weeks and two months old. Even if problems arise, the child is usually adoptable. Adoptive parents, however, need to be aware of the risks involved and the child's special needs before choosing to make a commitment to a particular child.

Do You Really Want to Adopt an Infant?

If you have thought about adopting a child, you may have imagined an infant like David as your own. Probably you are already aware that because of the widespread use of birth control, the availability of abortion, and the increasing acceptance of unmarried parenthood, it may be difficult to find a white, healthy newborn to adopt. Adoption agencies report that even the most qualified couples must usually wait at least a year and sometimes up to five years. But for minority families wanting to adopt minority children the situation is very different. If qualified, they usually find a baby in their arms within a year.

Think carefully about why an infant is important to you. An adoption agency will certainly ask you this. You may feel that by adopting an infant the child will be more your own. The child's first attachment will be to you. Parents who want to adopt infants often feel they will share in their children's development almost from the beginning, see them struggle to sit up, hear their first words, and watch them take their first steps. An infant will not have memories of other homes and will not have been hurt by experiences that occurred before living with you.

Adopting a child as an infant will not make him or her your birthchild. Sometimes people mistakenly believe that by adopting an infant the grown child will seem less "adopted." Of course this is not true. Whatever age children enter families, they still will be adopted.

You may reach the decision that you really want to adopt an infant. You realize that this baby will not be a substitute for a birthchild, but you want to experience raising a child from babyhood to adulthood. Listen to yourself. It is much better to endure a long wait or never adopt a child than out of desperation to adopt a child whom you don't feel you can love and accept.

How to Adopt an Infant or Young Child

Contact the state or county adoption agency and whatever private agencies service your community. (Refer to Chapter Five and the Appendix for assistance in locating agencies.) They may put you on a waiting list or ask you to file an application. *Make sure several agencies know of your interest in adopting a child.* Be persistent. Call every few months, letting them know that you still want to adopt a child. Many religious groups, for example Catholics, Mormons, and Jews, have adoption agencies. If your group has such an agency, apply through it. Some agencies with religious affiliation receive public funds and will provide you with services no matter what your religion is. Some people recommend applying to a Catholic agency as they may have more babies available.

You may want to consider an independent adoption — a non-agency adoption — if these in your state are legal. Your family, physician, attorney, or friends may know of parents wishing to relinquish a child. This is usually more risky than an agency adoption. Be sure to read Chapter Five before making a commitment.

Older Children

Six-year-old Paul lived with his mother, then with his grandmother, was placed for a year in a foster home, returned to his mother's care, was placed in a foster home again, then another, and now is awaiting placement in an adoptive home. Paul experienced six changes in caretakers and five different social workers.

Background and Risk Factors

Paul is an extreme example. However, most older children available for adoption have experienced foster care and changes in homes and caretakers. Usually a juvenile court, probation or welfare department, or social agency is responsible for the child. Their representative, most often a social worker, directly supervises the child's placement.

Perhaps the most dangerous result of frequent disruptions in a child's living situation is that he or she may not have had the opportunity to develop a crucial attachment to a *psychological parent* — a term used by professionals to describe the primary adult providing a child with day-to-day care, support, consistency, and nurturance. This attachment, usually formed in the first few years of life, is believed to form the basis for children's belief in their own worth, their trust in the world, and their ability to be intimate. Even if this attachment is disrupted or is less than ideal, it is better for a child to have made such an attachment than not. Some children are so damaged in early childhood that they are never able to tolerate the intimacy of close relationships or family.

Each time children change caretakers they must give up their reliance on the previous caretaker, (perhaps a psychological parent), try to make some sense of what is happening to them, and learn to live with and rely on new people. Social workers call this process "making separations." Children usually believe that they are more powerful than they are, and feel that they have brought about the changes by being bad, stupid, or unlovable. Even if Paul, mentioned above, can understand the reasons for the changes in his life, he will still feel pain, loss, sadness, apprehension, and discomfort in his new situation. With repeated separations children begin to expect failure and stop taking the risk of trusting and loving in new relationships. This can set up a pattern for future relationships and hinder the formation of ties with an adoptive family.

Paul will come to his adoptive home with six years prior experience. Already he will have developed interests, an attitude toward school, and an idea of what a family should be. He will also bring with him other things — memories of good times, special friends, arguments, perhaps a fear of dogs, a remembrance of being abused or neglected. All of these experiences, good and bad, will affect his adjustment to his adoptive family.

Most older children are able to weather previous experiences, separations, and disruptions. They flourish in their adoptive homes and grow into normal, caring adults. Whatever stresses an older child has experienced, the care and security of a stable home — the sooner the better — is usually the best remedy.

Children Adopted by Foster Parents

> Three years ago, Kathy, now ten, was placed by court order in the Gordon foster home. Initially her parents visited frequently, then contact lagged, and now her parents have agreed to relinquish her for adoption. In the past three years Kathy has developed a strong relationship with Mr. and Mrs. Gordon. The Gordons never expected Kathy's placement to be anything but temporary. When their two natural children became teenagers they began taking in foster children, both because they enjoyed children and to supplement their moderate income. The Gordons have grown to care for Kathy very much and now want to adopt her. They are legitimately concerned however, with the financial and other responsibilities of an "unplanned child."

The Gordons, like many foster parents, have through the years become the family and psychological parents of a child placed "temporarily" in their care. They have few legal rights to the child, they may be financially unable to support another child, and they may be at the stage of life where the responsibilities of another child are not totally welcome.

The Gordons and Kathy are fortunate. First, Kathy's birthparents agree to the adoption, and Kathy is protected by the court. Many foster parents are torn between their wish to adopt and their fear that if they initiate such action the birthparents, social worker, or court may remove the child. As a result, some foster parents, without the assistance of either the court or social agencies, informally care for a child for years. One such foster mother reports that she still regrets waiting so long to begin adoption proceedings because of these fears; for years her daughter never felt the security of really belonging.

Kathy's social worker and the court recognize the strength of her relationship with the Gordons and consider the Gordons the first choice as her adoptive parents. Some foster parents, particularly those with much younger foster children, find that the supervising agency plans to place the child with another family. If the foster family has a strong and lengthy relationship with the child, they may be able to contest this in court. The Gordons, however, were encouraged to adopt Kathy. To assist them, an adoption subsidy was arranged and the cost of the adoption itself was paid.

Adoption of Brothers and Sisters

> Kim, nine, Tina, five, and Heather, two, are half-sisters. There have been many ups and downs and changes in their lives, but they have almost always been together. Kim has been given a great deal of responsibility for her sisters' care. In new situations her sisters look to her for approval and to lead the way. All three girls have been freed for adoption. Their birthmother and the two older girls ask that they be placed together in an adoptive home.

Siblings (children sharing at least one parent) are placed in the same adoptive home whenever possible. Adoptees, particularly when they are adults, benefit by keeping ties with their biological siblings. Kim, Tina, and Heather, for example, feel security in their relationship. To break it would mean another loss for the girls.

Unfortunately, however, a large number of brothers and sister (six, for example) or an intense rivalry between the children make such a placement impossible.

Although it will be difficult, an attempt will be made to place Kim, Tina, and Heather together. They will need a rare, flexible, and understanding adoptive family. The impact of the introduction of three children in a home, all at the same time, is enormous. The adjustment will be difficult for everyone. The sisters are already a family, have already learned ways of getting along together, and initially will feel more loyalty to each other than to their adoptive family. Kim will most likely be reluctant to surrender her role as a "little mother." The younger two may feel they need Kim's approval in order to show affection to their adoptive parents. However, families who have adopted siblings report that in the end it was worth the trouble.

The Child's Need to Make Goodbyes to His or Her Birthfamily

> Anne is a solemn girl who seems older than her eight years. As both her parents were very young at the time of her birth, she was raised by her maternal grandmother. Three years ago her grandmother developed cancer. Anne remained with her grandmother until the latter's death, two years later, Anne's mother cared for her briefly, then placed her in a foster home. Both her birthparents have now decided to relinquish Anne for adoption.

There is more to ending a relationship than the death of one party or the stroke of a pen. It is above all an emotional process.

Before Anne can form a relationship with an adoptive family she needs to mourn the loss of her grandmother and parents, understand why they have left her, and accept their loss as permanent. If she does not do this she may feel responsible for the losses, expect rejection in another family, and fantasize that her birthparents will reclaim her.

Older children who are adopted through agencies usually have a social worker to help them separate from their birthfamilies. (If you are considering adopting an older child be sure to ask the agency how the child was helped to do this.) Anne's social worker recognized her sadness and encouraged her to talk about her parents and grandmother. Anne worried that had she perhaps helped her grandmother more, her grandmother would not have died. The social worker arranged for Anne and her mother to meet. The two of them looked over photographs together, and talked about Anne's grandmother. Anne's mother told her sadly but firmly that she could not give Anne the home, love, and caring that she needed. She felt the best way to be a mother to Anne now was to place her for adoption. (See Chapter Ten for a discussion of parting with an older child from the birthparent's perspective.)

The Child's Need to Participate in Making the Decision

Older children, with their own experiences and preferences, need to be participants in the decision about adoption. Their active cooperation is required in order for the adoption to be suc-

cessful. In some states, children between the ages of ten and fourteen have the right to refuse an adoption. (See Chapter Four, The
Legal Process.) Generally, though, even much younger children
are encouraged to help make decisions about their adoption.

When eight-year-old Anne was ready for adoption, her social
worker asked her to think about what sort of adoptive family she
would like. Would she like brothers and sisters? A quiet family?
She was reminded that there is no ideal family and that she should
concentrate on what was most important to her. After much discussion Anne requested that she be placed in a family with other
children. Her social workers felt Anne needed a family with her
religion, a family with two parents, and a family that would encourage her to act as a child. Anne was finally placed with the
Lloyds, a couple with two older children, and she is basking in the
luxury of being the family's "baby."

An Older Child Comes with a Past

An older child, like Anne, will remember his or her life before
entering the adoptive home. It will be obvious to Anne's new
school, friends, and relatives that she was not born eight years
old. She and the Lloyds will find themselves talking to outsiders
as well as to each other about her life before adoption. It is important to children to be comfortable in sharing past experiences —
whether they be memories of a trip to the mountains or of a dying
grandmother — with their adoptive families. Would-be adoptive
parents should ask themselves if they feel able to discuss any disturbing parts of a child's background with the child.

Why Adopt an Older Child?

Older children are more in need of adoptive homes and more
available for adoption than younger children. Moreover, many
families prefer to adopt an older child. You may be in your forties
or have a life style that does not lend itself to a totally dependent
newborn. Some parents, both birth and adoptive, find that they
enjoy their children more as they become older, more self-
reliant, and develop their own interests. Or, you may be one of
those adoptive parents who simply does not consider the child's
age to be a very important factor. You want a child in your life and
the experience of being a parent. If you decide to adopt an older
child you will need to be flexible enough to adjust to another
well-developed personality in your household, to reach out con-

siderably during the adjustment period, and to accept the child's early background, which may be very different from your own. (See Chapter Eight, The Adjustment Period, and Chapter Nine, The Adoptive Family through the Years.)

How to Adopt an Older Child

If you decide to adopt an older child who is not a relative, it is best to work with an adoption agency. This is important for several reasons. An adoption agency can provide you with a choice of children and information on their background and needs. A quiet, withdrawn child might be overwhelmed by some families but might blossom in your home. An older child usually finds it much more difficult to adjust than a younger child. An agency will help you get acquainted and provide the child with a safe link between his or her new and old homes. When problems arise — and they will — the agency will be a valuable resource for you and your child. Frequently older children are eligible for adoption subsidies, and an agency can help you secure this resource.

As most older children have been in foster care, a public agency will be responsible for the majority of them. Your county Welfare Department or Department of Social Services will refer you to the appropriate local agency. Tell them of your interest in adopting an older child. This will probably give you priority over other applicants.

Children with Special Needs

Robert, now almost nine months old, is a bright, attractive child born with a congenital defect in both feet. He underwent corrective surgery when he was two months old. He now wears casts on both legs, which because of rapid growth must be changed every few weeks. The casts and the surgery seem to have been effective in correcting the problem. However, Robert will need to wear the casts for at least three more months, after which he needs braces and perhaps further surgery. Robert will never be a track star. His doctor, though, expects that he will be able to walk unassisted by the age of five. Robert is awaiting placement in an adoptive home.

Robert is a basically healthy child with normal needs for love, stimulation, and fun. He will obviously make exceptional demands on his adoptive parents. In the past, children like Robert were often considered unadoptable. Most professionals now feel that it is essential for these children to have their own families. The frustrations of a physical or emotional difficulty are hard enough for a growing child without the additional handicap of not having a family. Robert's parents will need time, organizational ability, and — depending on where they live — considerable financial resources. Equally important, they will need the sensitivity to help Robert handle the fact that he is different from other children.

What Special Needs?

Generally, a child with special needs has a medical, genetic, emotional, developmental, or educational problem that requires additional care and understanding from the parents as well as adjustment and work from the child.

Robert, described above, has a correctable medical problem. Children are adopted with much more severe medical problems, such as blindness, deafness, cerebral palsy, heart defects, and diabetes. Other special needs include genetic problems, such as being a carrier of a hemophilia gene, emotional problems requiring continued psychiatric counseling, developmental disabilities, such as mild to moderate mental retardation, and learning disabilities or lags.

Children, like the rest of us, seldom fit into neat categories or are totally predictable. Often their special needs are the result of a combination of physical, emotional, and environmental factors that confound the precise diagnosis of the experts. Children's success in overcoming or living with their disabilities depends on their own perseverance and intelligence, the resources available in their communities, and the support of their families. Jane, described below, is an example.

> During her pregnancy, Jane's birthmother had little prenatal care. Jane was born underweight, one month premature, and required hospitalization for three weeks following her birth. She was removed from her mother's care when, at the age of a year and a half, she was left with a neighbor and developed a high fever. Since then she has lived in two foster homes and briefly with her mother. Her physical and intellectual development was slow. When she entered school, her teacher found her withdrawn and functioning well below the level of her peers. School testing showed her to have learning disabilities and an IQ of seventy (borderline mental retardation).

Jane is now free for adoption. In addition to being tested at school, she has been evaluated by a team consisting of a psychiatrist, medical doctors, a psychologist, and social workers. They agree that she is functioning well below the expected level for a child her age. They are not sure if this is the result of a genetic deficit, trauma at birth, medical problems, emotional problems, lack of stimulation, or a combination of many of these factors. These experts believe that Jane can at least achieve the social and vocational skills necessary to support herself as an adult. How much more is a guess. They are sure that the love and stability of a family are essential for her to realize whatever potential she has.

Why Adopt a Child with Special Needs?

Even though adoption agencies give priority to families wanting to adopt children with special needs, there are valid and realistic reasons not to adopt such a child. Often, in order to have any child, families try to be more flexible than they really are. Among the general reasons *not* to adopt a child with special needs are:

- These children usually require more time, money, and understanding than other children.
- Caring for these children can strain family and marital relationships.

A child with special needs would have difficulty in your home, if *you:*

- view adopting this child primarily as a charitable, romantic, or exciting act,
- would not want to be the parent of a normal child,
- have very high expectations for a child's performance,
- have difficulty dealing with change and stress.

Children with special needs are mostly just children. They misbehave, delight in their own accomplishments, argue, and need affection at odd times. If you enjoy children, want the challenge of raising a family, and look first at children's abilities and not at their disabilities, you may want to adopt a child with special needs. Children need to see themselves first as valuable and loved people and then realistically adjust to whatever handicap they have. If you view your child, for example, as a five-year-old boy with a problem in walking rather than as a cripple, he will be able to learn to feel the same way about himself.

In the case of kids with special needs it is often true that one man's meat is another man's poison. In some families a child's epilepsy is simply a manageable inconvenience, whereas in others it would be a tremendous embarrassment. It is important to remember that in adoption you do have a *choice*. Do not expect yourself to feel the same about every handicap. Look closely at your lifestyle, finances, educational expectations, and flexibility. You may find that the child others consider handicapped will be regarded as a child with a minor problem in your family.

How to Adopt a Child with Special Needs

You should work with an adoption agency. They will have evaluated the child and be able to give you a realistic appraisal of his or her problems and potential. An agency will also help you form a plan for the child's care and treatment before the adoption. They will assist in securing the financial, medical, educational, and psychiatric resources your child will need. Remember that children with special needs are likely to be eligible for adoption subsidies as well as financial assistance with the cost of treatment for medical conditions existing prior to the adoption. You may not want to be the parents of a child with a chronic medical problem and live 500 miles from the nearest source of treatment. Nor may you want to bankrupt yourself and your family in order to pay a child's medical bills. Be sure to check out the information the agency gives you with your own pediatrician, local schools, and other local resources before you decide to accept a child.

After you have decided to adopt a child with special needs, contact your local adoption agency. Indicate to them that you are interested in special needs children. Usually public adopotion agencies have more "special needs" children. After the agency has completed your homestudy — an in depth evaluation of your suitability as adoptive parents — you may want to register with one of the national adoption pools, ARENA (Adoption Resource Exchange of North America) or AASK (Aid to Adoption of Special Kids). This will increase the possibilities of your being matched with such a child. (See Chapter Five, the section, "Services to Adoptive Parents.")

The Minority or Racially Mixed Child

Professionals in the adoption field do not use a child's adoptive placement as a means to make a social statement. They consider the law (some states do not allow transracial adoptions), the attitudes of the community, and the preferences of the birthparents, and then they try to make the adoptive placement that is in the best interests of the child and the adoptive parents.

Adoption professionals usually wish to place minority children with adoptive families of their own race for a number of reasons. One's race, like one's sex, is part of one's identity for life. Minority children must contend with their differentness as well as with discrimination, and then develop a positive sense of themselves and their race. Professionals feel that parents of the same minority group can best help their children do this. They themselves are models for their children, and they have already experienced the struggles their children will encounter.

For these reasons adoption agencies now recruit minority families for minority children. For such families, adoption procedures are almost exactly the same as they are for other families. The difference is that for these families adoption is usually easier and quicker, and they are more likely to be able to adopt an infant.

Transracial adoptions, those in which the child and parents are of different races, are usually considered only when an agency is unable to find appropriate adoptive parents of the child's own race or racial mixture. But professionals feel that a secure and loving relationship with an adult is a child's most basic need, and adoption agencies generally do not find enough minority or racially mixed homes in which to place the minority children under their care. As a result, they sometimes place children transracially, believing that even if the children experience problems they are better off having parents of a different race than having no parents.

Rules for the Racial Match Game

All things being equal, adoption agencies try to match the racial background of the adoptive family with the racial background of the birthfamily. It seems ridiculous today to place a child on a color wheel and attempt to match shades, but it does seem to make a difference, and it matters to the children and families involved. Families live in communities — not just on love alone. The rules seem to vary somewhat with the different racial groups.

The black or part-black child. Generally a child who appears at all black is considered black by his community. Transracial adoptions are most difficult for the child. If black parents are not available, an agency will try to place with a family having some black or minority members.

The Asian or part-Asian child. In many communities the Asian or part-Asian child is considered almost "white," and is easily adopted by and assimiliated into Caucasian families.

The Hispanic or part-Hispanic child. Hispanic children, particularly if they are light-skinned, are regularly adopted by Caucasian families and accepted in predominantly white communities.

The Indian or part-Indian child. Until recently, Indian children were encouraged to leave their tribal and family groups on reservations and grow up in institutions, foster homes, and adoptive homes. This drained Indians of their most valuable resource, their children, and often produced an adult who was cultureless and without family or tribal ties. For most Caucasian families there are few emotional barriers to their adopting an Indian or part-Indian child. However, Indian groups are strongly resistive to this. Federal legislation enacted in May, 1979 will severely limit the adoption of full or part-Indians by non-Indians.

Transracial Adoptions

> John is an active thirteen-month-old child who is walking just enough to get into everything he shouldn't. His birth-parents are a young, unmarried, black and white couple who relinquished him for adoption shortly after his birth. John has a significant hearing loss that will require further evaluation, medical treatment, and perhaps speech therapy. His adoption agency has been unable to find black or black-white adoptive parents willing to take on the responsibilities of John's condition. As the agency feels John should not wait much longer for an adoptive placement, a white family is being considered.

In most transracial adoptions the adoptive parents are Caucasian and the child is of a minority background. This is the result of a surplus of both Caucasian adoptive families and adoptable minority children.

It is one thing to believe intellectually, politically, or morally that any child, regardless of race, is equal and valuable. It is another to have the ability to love and make your own a child of a different racial background. In order for John's adoption to be successful his adoptive parents will need this ability. Finding this out is a difficult task for anyone.

It is helpful to examine your motives for wanting a racially dif-

ferent child. If you believe that you are making a courageous social statement, doing the right thing, taking a stand against racial
prejudice, or making up for past wrongs, you are thinking about
causes — not children. Think in terms of what you can give a child
and what he or she can give you.

Some practical ways to discover if you want to adopt a child
transracially are to talk with other parents who have adopted children of other races and to get to know families and children of
minority backgrounds. If you do decide to adopt a minority child,
these people can be a support group for you and your child.

A white family that adopts a racially different child is never totally white again. Both the child and the family will experience
and have to contend with whatever stereotypes and racial prejudices exist in the community. The family — parents and children
— cannot rely on the neighborhood to approve of them or their
adopted child.

It is much easier for a family to adopt transracially if their relatives, social group, neighborhood, and community are racially
mixed and accept differences. There are times when any child dislikes being different. Being the only black or Asian child in a
school puts a child continually on display. Children who live in a
community where some of their friends, teachers, and neighbors
are of their racial background can be just kids rather than, say, the
Jones' adopted black child.

Children of transracial adoptions need exposure and contact
with people of their own racial and cultural backgrounds in order
to provide them with models and give them an understanding of
their own biological and cultural heritage. If these people can be
found in the community or among the parents' friends, it is much
easier for the family. Some families need to create these contacts
for their children, and, for example, join a church that has members of their child's race.

How to Adopt a Minority or Racially Mixed Child

There is seldom a reason not to take advantage of the services of
an adoption agency. These children are available. If you are
adopting transracially you will want to use the counseling services
an agency will provide. And an agency will help you in securing
adoption subsidies, if available.

Part II
Acting on the Decision

Four:
The Legal Process

In General

Adoption legally results in a complete substitution of parents for the adopted child. Unlike guardianship, which only suspends the rights and duties of natural parents, adoption permanently cuts off the natural parents' legal relationships with the child.

The effect of a legal adoption is perhaps best explained by a typical adoption law (in this case a California law):

> A child, when adopted, may take the family name of the person adopting. After adoption, the two shall sustain towards each other the legal relation of parent and child, and have all the rights and duties of that relation. The parents of an adopted child are, from the time of adoption, relieved of all parental duties towards, and all responsibility for, the child so adopted, and have no right over it.
>
> (Calif. Civ. C. §§228, 229)

Generally an adopted child has all the rights of a natural child, including in some instances the right of inheritance through the adoptive parents. (See the section, "The Child's Right of Inheritance," in this chapter.)

How the Courts Interpret the Laws

The adoption laws in the various states differ in many respects. Still, where there is a controversy about an adoption proceeding judges will almost uniformly apply the laws so as to (1) promote the welfare of the child and (2) support the rights of the natural parents.

☑ Note: These rules, which lawyers and judges call "rules of construction," are only important where the law is unclear or where there is something to be said (legally) for both sides of the dispute. Otherwise, of course, the laws will be applied as they are written.

Who May Adopt

In the majority of states, the person adopting a child must be an adult (from eighteen to twenty-one years old, depending on the state), who is a resident of the state in which the adoption proceedings begin. Other states differ on the residency requirement, as outlined below.

Residency Requirements

In those states which require the adopting person to be a "resident" of the state in which the legal proceedings for adoption begin, most judges insist that the adopting person actually live in the state — not just temporarily arrange an address there. Some judges even require that the adopting person have maintained a home and been physically present in the state for a given period of time before they file for adoption. Residence requirements may be complicated, and obviously any prospective adopting parent should have his or her state's laws explained carefully by a lawyer or the agency handling the adoption.

Age Requirements

As stated above, the adopting person must be an adult. The states differ, however, on other age requirements. For example, some states require that the adopting person be a given number of years (usually about ten) older than the person adopted. Stepparent adoptions are usually exempt from such age requirements (see below). Other states simply require that the person adopting be of a certain age or older. Reminder: The age of the adopting person may be important in another legal sense at the hearing on the adoption application. Judges are permitted to consider the ages of both the adopting parent and the child in making their decision as to what is in the best interest of the child. For example, if the person seeking the adoption is of a very advanced age and the child is very young, these facts, together with other circumstances, may result in the application being denied.

Race or Religion

Some states still have laws forbidding interracial adoptions, although the trend is to hold such laws unconstitutional (as in Texas, for example). In those states which have no express laws on this point, a judge may not deny an adoption application *solely* because the child and adopting parent are of different races. Remember, though, that race — like almost all other factors — can be considered by a judge in determining what is in the best interests of the child. But if you feel, as a prospective adopting parent, that your adoption application was denied only because of racial differences, contact your lawyer and fight it!

The laws in some states specify that insofar as is practicable older children should be placed for adoption with adoptive parents of the same religious faith. Judges regard these laws as merely advisory rather than as legal requirements. Many other states have no laws at all on this point, and in most cases religion alone is not a critical issue in the legal proceedings.

Prior Relationship to the Child

The right of grandparents to adopt their grandchild is universally recognized. Such adoptions are very common in situations where the grandchild already lives with the grandparents and the natural mother is unable or unwilling to care for the child. These adoptions usually present few legal difficulties.

Likewise, stepparent adoptions are common and are highly favored by the courts. The only major legal problem involved in stepparent adoptions generally is that involving consent, which is discussed in detail below.

Who May Be Adopted

The great majority of adoptions are of minor children, and most of the legal procedure is designed for such adoptions. However, most states also permit the adoption of adults. Note that a married minor may be adopted in practically all of the states. Special laws, such as those in California, provide for the adoption of hard-to-place children. (These laws are discussed in Chapters Three and Five.)

Noncitizen Children

In those states which follow the Uniform Adoption Act, any child may be adopted who is in the state when the adoption proceedings are begun — regardless of his or her residency or citizenship. And in states that do not follow the act, adoption of alien children is generally permitted if the child can be brought into the court's jurisdiction, namely, the area in which the court has the power to make judgments. (Intercountry or foreign adoptions are discussed in Chapter Seven.) We recommend that if you are considering such an adoption you seek help from the U.S. Immigration and Naturalization Service, as well as from your state agency regulating such adoptions. (See Chapter Seven.)

Blood Relations

As stated above, grandparent adoptions are permitted. Where a state's laws do not forbid adoptions between blood relations, an adoption may even take place in cases where the relation of parent and child already exists. This is true in Tennessee, for example, where a natural mother of an illegitimate child was permitted to legally adopt the child later. And in Kentucky a husband was permitted to legally adopt his wife as his child and heir at law. Caution: In states where such adoptions are not prohibited, a mother, divorced from her husband, cannot legally adopt her own child so as to cut off his or her natural relationship to the father.

Frequently, blood relationship adoptions are undertaken for the purpose of making the adopted person eligible to inherit property. Such adoptions are valid provided they conform to the laws of the state in which they take place.

Adoption Contracts

A legal adoption must take place under the laws of the state in which the petition or application for adoption is filed. Still, most states recognize and honor private contracts or agreements to adopt a child, provided the contract is between adults.

In all states, however, it is a crime to pay or offer money to the parent of a child for (1) placement for adoption, (2) his or her consent to adoption, or (3) cooperation in completing the adoption of his or her child. Distinction: It is a common, acceptable practice for an adoptive parent to offer medical care and the like to a pregnant woman who is placing her child with the former for adoption. This does not violate the law in most states. The same is generally true of legal costs paid by the adoptive parents. (See Chapter Six for further discussion.)

Any contract must be supported by what judges and lawyers call "consideration." This means simply that something of value must be given in exchange for the promise of the other person. In adoption contracts, such consideration may be the giving up of the natural parent of the right to the child and his or her companionship, in return for the other party taking on parental duties.

Enforcement

Just like any other contract or agreement that is legally binding, adoption contracts will be enforced by the court if one party fails to perform his or her part of the agreement. In many cases, damages have been awarded for breach of an adoption agreement since a judge will seldom compel the parties to go ahead with the adoption, because of the sensitive nature of adoption.

Anyone claiming that such a contract has been breached by the other person must, of course, offer proof that the agreement was made. Such proof in most cases is obviously the written agreement itself. In some cases, though, judges have determined that the agreement was oral only but have still enforced it.

If the natural parent who agreed to give up his or her child for adoption has died before the agreement could be completed, the court will usually compel that person's estate (heirs at law) to perform the agreement. On the other hand, if the prospective adoptive parent has died before the agreement could be completed, the courts probably will not try to enforce the agreement unless the deceased adoptive parent had promised the natural parent that the child would be included in the former's will.

In some states, severe misbehavior of the child may be grounds for canceling the agreement, but in most cases a bargain is a bargain and it stands. But like any other legal contract, if false representations have been made the other party may cancel the contract. For example, if the natural parent has said that the child has no medical history of serious disease and it turns out later that the child has suffered brain damage from a prior disease, the adoptive parents have a good chance of rescinding (canceling) the agreement.

Checklist of Matters to Be Included

In all instances, we recommend that a lawyer or an experienced adoption specialist draw up adoption agreements for independent adoptions. The following checklists of matters to be included or considered in an independent adoption agreement may nevertheless be of assistance when considering such an agreement.

- Person being adopted:
  — name

— age
— date of birth
— place of birth
— sex
— religion
— race
— property owned
- Adoptive parent or parents:
— name
— address
— age
— marital status
— competency
— religion
— race
— relationship to person being adopted, if any
- Natural (birth) parents:
— names
— addresses
— marital status
— consent to adoption
— authorization for adoptive parents to obtain child's medical history
- Date of agreement

Consent of Persons Involved

This chapter discusses the legal considerations involved in obtaining the consent of (1) the child's natural parent or parents, (2) the child, where this is necessary, and (3) the adoptive parents or parent.

Consent from the required persons will generally be obtained by private lawyers or experienced adoption agency personnel, and, in most cases, the persons involved in the adoption need not worry about the legality of the consent obtained. Still, a prospective adoptive parent, a natural parent considering adoption of his or her child, or even the child, when old enough, should acquaint themselves with the basic legal principles involved. The subject of consent probably presents the chief legal problem involved in adoptions.

The Child

The consent of a child to his or her adoption is required in most states if the child is over a given age. Usually this age is from twelve to fourteen. The child's consent is usually obtained by the judge hearing the adoption proceedings.

The Adopting Parents

The consent of the adopting parents is, of course, required for a valid adoption. Ordinarily, this consent is made in writing when the adopting parents file their petition or application for adoption. If only one person from a married couple makes the application, most states require that person to obtain the consent of his or her spouse unless the couple are legally separated.

Suppose a married couple makes an application for an adoption, the legal proceedings commence, and then the couple are separated or divorced before the adoption is final. In this situation, most courts will stop the adoption proceedings unless the best interests of the child demand otherwise.

The Natural Parents

Universally, the consent of a child's natural parents to its adoption is required unless (1) they have lost their parental rights through legal proceedings of (2) they have abandoned or deserted the child. Both of these exceptions are discussed below.

The right to give or withhold consent to the adoption of a child is based on the right of custody of the child. Natural parents acquire custodial rights at the child's birth and retain these rights until the child comes of age or until the parents lose their custodial rights. In the latter case, a guardian is usually appointed to act for the child and the guardian's consent must be obtained.

Single Parent. Obviously, where the natural parent is a widow or widower the consent of the deceased spouse is legally dispensed with. Where the natural parents are divorced or legally separated, the rules in the various states are different. In some states, the consent of both parents is still required even though custody of the child has been awarded to one of the parents. In other states, probably the majority, only the consent of the parent to whom custody has been awarded is necessary.

☑ Caution: In practically all states, the terms of the divorce or separation decree are important in that they may provide for the giving or withholding of such consent. Furthermore, such decrees often contain temporary provisions affecting custody of the child, and this too may affect the necessity for consent.

Some states have special rules governing the necessity of con-

sent when a noncustodial parent has failed to observe the terms of
the divorce or separation decree. In California, for example, if the
noncustodial parent has failed for one year or more to pay ordered
child support or visit the child, his or her consent to the child's
adoption is no longer required. If you are a custodial parent considering adoption and your ex-spouse has failed in the above regards, contact your lawyer or the adoption agency with whom you
are working to find out whether this is true in your state.

Parent(s) of Illegitimate Children: The Changing Law. First, the
mother of an illegitimate child must consent to the child's adoption in all states. *This is true even if the mother is a minor.* The
only exceptions to this rule are (1) where the mother is legally unable to give such consent because she is incompetent, (2) where
she has abandoned the child and her parental rights have been
terminated (see below), and (3) where she has voluntarily turned
over the child to an adoption agency and relinquished control of
it.

In some states, the consent of the father of an illegitimate child
is not required for its adoption unless the father has acknowledged his paternity and married the mother of the child. This is
true, for example, in states that follow the Uniform Adoption Act.
In these states, the father of such a child must receive notice of the
adoption proceedings and is entitled to contest them if he desires.
In short, where the father legitimatizes the child by later marrying the mother, most states recognize his legal interest in the
adoption proceedings.

The above law, however, is now subject to a recent (April,
1979) decision by the United States Supreme Court that deals
specifically with the rights of an unmarried father as regards the
adoption of his child. The case deals with a New York couple (unmarried) who had a child that the mother later sought to have
adopted by the child's new stepfather, without the consent of the
natural father.

In its decision, the Supreme Court held that the adoption
should not proceed without the right of the father to contest it in
state court. The Court did *not* hold that the adoption must fail in
the absence of the father's consent, but *did* give him the right to
oppose it on whatever grounds he might have.

Since the law as stated by the United States Supreme Court
must be followed by all state courts, this recent decision will affect
the laws of all states as regards the rights of unmarried fathers to
their children — even though the father might be separated from

the child's mother. By the time this text is published, this decision will have been studied carefully by everyone interested or involved in adoptions and parental rights generally. Needless to say, if you are involved at all in the adoption of an illegitimate child (in any capacity), be sure to check with your agency or lawyer as to the effect of this decision.

When Consent Is Not Required: Abandonment of the Child. A natural parent may, by neglect of the child or other circumstances, forfeit his or her parental rights; thereby the child may be adopted without his or her consent. *However, the parent's rights to the child must have been terminated in a legal proceeding.* Otherwise, the parent has not been given what the lawyers call "due process of law," and he or she can later annul the adoption.

The "neglect or other circumstances" referred to above usually means abandonment of the child. Although it is difficult to define abandonment precisely, you may think of it as any conduct showing that the parent intends to give up all parental duties and relinquish all claims to the child. In other words, the parent has forsaken the child and abdicated his or her responsibility to it.

Abandonment does *not* mean that the parent, through circumstances, is unable to support the child. Nor does the parent's inability to physically care for the child, because of the parent's sickness, constitute abandonment of the child. The following, however, are considered by most judges to be abandonment of a child:

- leaving a child in the care of others permanently or indefinitely
- consistent, willful failure to support and care for a child
- surrender of a child to a hospital, physician, or the like with intent to surrender parental rights
- physical desertion of a child, where the parent does not know of the child's whereabouts for a long period (usually one year)

As we said above, even though a parent has abandoned or deserted a child, the parent's rights must be legally terminated before his or her consent to adoption is not required. Termination, in this sense, does not mean that the child has been temporarily taken from the parent, as may be the case when juvenile authorities have the child in custody.

Tommy, the son of Pete and Alice, received pretty shabby treatment at home, was expelled from school, and ran away.

When found, he was taken to the juvenile authorities as a runaway. Custody of Tommy still remains with his parents, and should the question of adoption arise their consent will be needed.

Jane's parents spend more time drinking and fighting than caring for Jane. She left home some time ago and lives with her boyfriend. Recently she became involved in some heavy drug problems, was declared to be a ward of the court, and placed in a foster home. Her foster parents (brave souls) want to adopt her but will need her parents' consent since a proceeding to declare a child a ward of the court does not permanently terminate parental rights.

As a result of parental abuse, Dave developed an antisocial mean streak and twice was incarcerated at juvenile hall for injuring other children. After the third episode, the court ordered a hearing on the matter of Dave's custody and the termination of his parents' rights, at which Dave's parents were present. Their parental rights were terminated, and Dave was placed in the custody of foster parents. Should they want to adopt Dave, his parents' consent will not be required.

Incompetent Parent. A person who is legally incompetent (called insane in some states) cannot give his or her legal consent to the adoption of a child. If a guardian has been appointed for such a person, the guardian may usually give consent (provided that the judge is satisfied the adoption is in the best interests of both the parent and the child). If a guardian for the person has not been appointed, then in most cases one will be appointed for the purpose of the adoption.

☑ Note: The above rules do not apply to natural parents who are eccentric and perhaps considered "crazy" by their neighbors. To have a guardian appointed for purposes of adoption, they must have been *legally found* to be incompetent.

The Guardian or Representative

The laws in most states provide for the consent to a child's adoption by his or her legal representative where the child's natural parents are deceased or have relinquished or forfeited their parental rights. Usually this legal representative is the child's legal guardian, who may be related to the child (such as a grandparent) or not.

Sometimes a guardian may be appointed for the child for the

purpose of the adoption itself. Where this is true, most courts have the power to order that the guardian consent to the adoption. In other states, the courts have the power to declare that the guardian's consent is not essential to the adoption if the guardian refuses, without reason, to consent to the adoption.

Institution or Agency. In most states, when a child has been placed in an institution or child-care agency, the consent of the institution or agency to the child's adoption must be obtained. Usually such consent is part of the placement procedure. On the other hand, if the agency is a private institution (such as a private orphans' home) consent must be obtained — in writing.

In some cases, the institution or agency (such as a public welfare agency) is also the guardian of the child, and their consent is given in their capacity as guardian.

Foster Parents. Although foster parents do not have the rights of adoptive parents, nevertheless they have often cared for the child for some time and in many instances have formed a close relationship with the child.

Some states, recognizing the interest of the foster parents in the adoption procedure, have enacted laws that require the consent of foster parents to the adoption of the child in their care. In other states, foster parents have standing in court (are authorized) to contest adoption of their foster child if they feel it is not in the child's best interest.

Withdrawal of Consent

In most states, where the consent of the natural parents is required, the consent must be in writing, signed and delivered to the proper person (court, agency head, and so on). Such a consent may ordinarily *not* be withdrawn by the natural parents except with court approval.

Where the consent was obtained by fraud or by misrepresentation, the court will, of course, annul or cancel the consent. Otherwise, each case depends on its facts.

> A sixteen-year-old unwed mother signed a consent to adoption of her child after a full discussion of her rights and the law with a doctor, a representative of a social work department, her mother, and others. Subsequently she asked the court to annul her consent on the grounds that she was unaware of its consequences. Her request was denied.
>
> A pregnant mother was divorced just before her child was

born. Although very emotionally upset, she consented to
adoption of the child and received little if any advice from
anyone as to the proceedings. Later, her request to withdraw her consent was granted by the court.

Even where the person seeking to withdraw consent is not able
to demonstrate clearly to a judge that he or she legally has sufficient grounds for withdrawal of consent, the judge may still approve such a withdrawal if it appears to be in the best interests of
the child. This principle — the discretion of the judge to order
what is best for the child — runs through all the legal adoption
proceedings and controls most if not all of the judge's decisions in
any case.

☑ Warning: If the adoption has proceeded rather far and all of
the parties involved (including the child) are depending on it
going through, the courts are less inclined to grant permission to
withdraw consent — at least in the absence of outright fraud or
the like. The point? Be sure, when you sign a consent, that you
are aware of the consequences of it. You may be unable to change
your mind later. The circumstances under which a completed
adoption may be annulled are discussed below.

The Court Hearing

The procedures and considerations leading up to an adoption
hearing (the application, investigation, and so on) are discussed in
Chapters Five and Six. The following deals with the legal aspects
of an adoption hearing before a judge.

Who Must Attend

The adoptive parents and the child to be adopted must ordinarily appear in court for the hearing — with their lawyer or adoption
agency representative where one or the other is involved. If one
of the adoptive parents is in the military service they may make
their appearance through a lawyer or other representative.

The states differ as to whether the above requirements are ab-
solute. In some states, no one need appear at the hearing provided all the necessary papers have been filed with the judge. In
other states, the presence of the child is not always required (unless he or she is over a given age and must consent verbally to the
adoption in court). Your lawyer or agency representative will, of
course, advise you whether your appearance will be required.

Where and How the Hearing Is Conducted

In almost every state, hearings on adoption petitions or applications are private, with only the required court personnel present in addition to the parties and the judge. Usually, adoption hearings are conducted in the judge's private chambers and are very informal. There is no need to be apprehensive about these court appearances. They are not a trial, and in almost all instances the judge will be friendly but firm in questioning you. But you need not feel that you will be cross-examined — the questions are merely to make sure all is in order and that the interests of the child are being served.

Report of Expenses and Costs

In the majority of states, the persons petitioning for the adoption must file in court a statement that contains the following:

- all expenses in connection with the birth, placement, care of the mother and child, and so on
- an itemization of all services rendered in connection with the adoption, including the dates of payments
- the names and addresses of the lawyers, doctors, licensed adoption agencies, or other persons handling or receiving money paid out by the adoptive parents

The purpose of this report is to ensure that the judge can determine the adoption is legal and is not a black market or gray market adoption disguised as something else. (See Chapter Six.) The statement is submitted to the judge for approval under penalty of perjury.

Matters Considered by the Judge

As always, the judge will be guided by the best interests of the child in examining the papers and the persons present at the hearing. In addition to this paramount principle, the judge will consider, where appropriate:

- the age of the adoptive parents
- the age of the child
- the race and religion of the child and the adoptive parents
- the financial background and present status of the adoptive parents
- the wishes of the child (depending on his or her age)
- the reports and recommendations of the agencies involved

Child to Remain in County during the Adoption

Many states forbid the adoptive parents (or anyone else) from hiding a child or removing a child from the county where the adoption proceedings are being held, after the adoption has begun.

These states usually have exceptions to the above rule. Typical among these are the following situations:

- where the adoptive parents apply for and receive court permission to remove the child from the county
- where the child's absence will be less than a specified short time (usually thirty days)
- where stepparents are adopting and the child is in their custody
- where the child has been returned to the custody of the natural parents
- where the child has been relinquished for adoption to a county adoption agency and the latter obtains approval from the appropriate state agency

Approval or Disapproval of the Adoption

When satisfied as to all the pertinent information, the judge will either sign an adoption decree (sometimes called judgment or order) or deny the petition or application. If it is denied, the persons petitioning for the adoption have a right to appeal the judge's decision. This, of course, requires legal assistance.

If the judge signs the decree, the legal relationship of parent and child is established between the child and its new parents. The decree is usually in the child's *adopted name,* not in his or her prior name.

If the adoptive parents so request, the clerk of the court will generally issue them a certificate of adoption that includes the following:

- the date and place of adoption
- the child's birthday
- the name of the adopting parents
- the name the child has taken

When the adoption decree is entered in the court's records, in most states the clerk of the court sends a form to the state's registrar and a new birth certificate is prepared for the child. A fee of about five dollars is usually required (per adopted person).

A single parent adopting a child may request in most states that the adoption certificate reflect his or her single parent status. And in some states, when the adoption is by a surviving married person, that person may request that the adoption certificate name his or her deceased spouse as a parent of the child.

Also, on the request of the adoptive parents, the certificate may be amended to omit the name of the place where the child was born and the color or race of the parents (where that has been included). And in some states (such as California) the adopting parents may even have the child's city and county of birth deleted from the certification of adoption.

☑ Recommendation: Talk with your lawyer or representative about your wishes in the above matters *before* you go to the hearing. Once the decree and certificate are prepared, they may be difficult to change.

Note: In stepparent adoptions, many of the above procedures are dispensed with or shortened. In such adoptions — particularly where the stepparents already have custody of the child — there is less need for a full legal inquiry into the circumstances of the persons involved.

Nullifying Adoptions

It is, of course, important to all the persons involved in the adoption to know when the decree of adoption is "final," in the sense that the parties are assured of its permanency. The following discusses the circumstances under which an adoption decree may be nullified (that is, annulled, set aside, or canceled) by a court.

Lack of Notice to and Consent of the Natural Parents

As stated above, the most common legal problem encountered in adoptions involves the consent or lack of consent of the natural parents. In any adoption proceeding where the natural parents have failed to be informed of the adoption petition or have not given their consent to the adoption (where consent is required — see above), they may apply to have the adoption annulled.

The same rule applies where the child's guardian has not been notified or consented to the adoption.

Fraud, Undue Influence, or Mistake

Where the consent of the natural parents (or the guardian) of the child was obtained by fraud or illegal pressure (undue influence), they may start court proceedings to annul the adoption.

> A father leaving for military service consented to the adoption of his daughter on the representations of the adoptive parents' lawyer that it was necessary to protect the child; he was told she would be returned to him on his return from overseas. When he returned and the adoptive parents refused to relinquish the child, the father brought a successful court action to annul the adoption.

> A mother signed a consent to adoption form because she was told that it was necessary to permit her child to inherit from his grandparents. Later, on learning the falsity of the representation, she successfully had the adoption annulled.

> A mother was persuaded to sign a consent to adoption paper on the basis that the paper was only necessary to correct the child's birth certificate. She did not appear in court at the adoption proceedings because she was told that it was not necessary to do so. Later, a court annulled the adoption because of the misrepresentations.

> A mother's lawyer, who had arranged all the details of the adoption of her child, induced the child's father to sign a consent agreement by telling the father that the child would be adopted even without the father's consent, and that if he did not sign his wife would not reconcile with him. The lawyer also told the father that in any event the adoption would not be final for six months and that during that time it could be canceled. The court later allowed the father to revoke the adoption.

There are, of course, many more illustrations of situations in which an adoption may be revoked, and the above are only examples.

A Defective Child

In most states, the law provides that where an adopted child shows evidence of a mental deficiency or mental illness, resulting from a condition that existed before the child's adoption, the adoptive parents may ask the court to annul or set aside the adoption. One condition of this rule, however, is that the adoptive parents must not have known of the child's condition at the time of adoption.

The usual way in which a judge determines whether the child's condition fits within the rule is by deciding whether the child's condition would make him or her "unadoptable" by an agency.

The natural parents may have practiced fraud or made misrepresentations in connection with the child's medical history. If this is the case, then the court will be even more inclined to grant the adoptive parents' request to annul the adoption. (On the medical examination of a prospective adoptee, see Chapter Five.)

Time Limits for Nullification

Even when fraud is practiced on the adoptive parents, they must request that the adoption be nullified within a certain time in almost all states. This time may vary from three to five years. If you want to nullify an adoption, however, you would be well advised to start legal action as soon as possible after you discover the grounds justifying such action. Legally, if you wait too long to act — after you discover the true facts — a judge may decide that your delay has caused too much trouble for everyone and refuse you request.

Rights and Duties after Adoption

As stated earlier in this chapter, a child, when adopted, has the same legal relationship to his adoptive parents — and them to him — as their natural child would have. The new parents now have the following rights:

- the right to exclusive custody of the child
- the right to the child's earnings
- the right to control the child's education
- the right to the child's services

Conversely, the following duties are among those assumed by the new parents:

- the duty to support the child
- the duty to educate and raise the child in a proper manner
- the duty to abide by the terms of the adoption decree or agreement

The Child's Right of Inheritance

Although the laws in the various states differ, the tendency of modern property law is to give an adopted child the same right as a natural child to inherit from the adoptive parents. On the other hand, most laws take away the adopted child's right to inherit from his or her natural parents in the same manner as would their natural children.

In many states, however, adopted children retain the right to inherit through their natural parents unless they are specifically disinherited. And when children are adopted after their natural parents' death, they usually retain the right of natural inheritance even after their adoption.

Property laws are complex in every state, and inheritance laws involving adoption are even more complex. Little purpose would be served by attempting to summarize or even list here the various states' laws and their effects on adopted children and their new parents.

☑ Recommendation: After you have completed an adoption (if not before), consult your lawyer about your will, property status, and so on. This is *very important* and may be overlooked in the day-to-day details of your new family. If you fail to do this, the disposition of your property may not be as you would wish it.

Five:
Agency Adoptions

In General

Most birthparents and adoptive parents use the services of adoption agencies. We, the authors, believe that for birthparents, adoptive parents, and especially children there are few good reasons not to use an adoption agency, except where a relationship between the adoptive parent and child already exists.

This is debatable of course. Many advocates of independent adoptions point to very successful nonagency adoptions. However, we think the benefits of the counseling, evaluation, and procedural safeguards that agencies provide outweigh most advantages of independent adoption. (This will be discussed in depth in Chapter Six, Nonagency Adoptions.)

In this chapter you will find a description of the mechanics of an agency adoption and the services agencies usually provide for birthparents, adoptive parents, and children.

What is an Adoption Agency?

A state-licensed adoption agency provides adoption services to birthparents, adoptive parents, and children. Usually these services include:

- counseling
- evaluation and screening
- transfer of a child from birthparents to appropriate adoptive parents
- legally freeing a child for adoption

Many adoption agencies cling to a traditional view of family life. Generally speaking, adoption services developed in a time of different social values — a time when abortion was illegal, nonmarital births unacceptable, single parenthood unusual, and the rights of unmarried fathers minimal. As a result of this legacy many agencies view a "Pop at the office, Mom at home with the kids family" as best for children.

Adoption professionals are prone to believe that adoption will best meet a child's needs. Most of them have known children who were severely damaged by poor parenting and by birthparents whose lives were disrupted by an unwanted child. A major satisfaction of their job is the vicarious joy they experience in placing a child with an adoptive family. Also, private agencies usually rely on adoptive placements and the fees they generate in order to exist.

Adoption agencies have other biases. Almost any agency will consider the child's welfare first. Agencies do not exist to find babies for childless couples or to give birthparents the opportunity to relieve themselves of responsibility. *You do not have the right to adopt a child or to surrender your child for adoption.* Agencies arrange for adoption when they feel a child is adoptable and adoption is best for the child.

Most agencies reflect the values of their communities and their affiliation. A public adoption agency may be anxious to place tax-supported foster children for adoption. A Catholic agency, on the other hand, is unlikely to give you abortion counseling.

You, the birthparents and prospective adoptive parents, are the consumers of adoption services. You can expect an adoption agency to treat you courteously and to explain their decisions and practices. How they treat you will be a good indication of the care they generally use. You should question an agency that is too willing to accept a child for adoption or to give you a child. It is important to you that the interests of all parties to the adoption — the birthparents, the adoptive parents, and the child — are protected and that all receive the appropriate care, evaluation, and counseling.

How to Find an Adoption Agency

In your area you will find at least one public agency providing adoption services. In addition there may be private agencies, perhaps one affiliated with your religious group. All licensed adoption agencies in your state will be registered with your state licensing agency. (See appendix.) You can write and request the names and addresses of your local agencies.

Your local Welfare Department or Department of Social Services should be able to refer you to the public adoption agency serving your community. Other agencies may be listed in the Yellow Pages of your telephone directory under "Adoption Services."

The Social Worker

Betty Reynolds has been a social worker at Bundle of Joy Adoption Agency for the last five years. She is forty-seven, married, and the mother of two children, the youngest of whom is still at home. After she finished college she married and began raising her family. As her children approached their teens she became restless; she decided to return to college and get a master's degree in social work. She is happy with her job at Bundle of Joy but sometimes feels overworked and tired of other people's problems. Occasionally she wonders why her husband refuses to balance a checkbook and worries if her son will ever develop more interests in life than dirt bikes.

Generally, the representative of an adoption agency who provides supervision and counseling services is a social worker. Occasionally a psychologist, a probation officer, a minister, or another counselor will function in the same capacity. Agency staff often includes a nurse, a physician, a psychiatrist, and an attorney. The social worker usually has three functions:

- providing counseling and services to birthparents
- evaluating and counseling prospective adoptive parents
- counseling and supervising children under the agency's care

In some agencies one social worker will do all three jobs, in others a different person performs each function.

Most social workers have advanced training in human psychology, human development, and counseling. They may or may not have a master's degree in social work (M.S.W.).

Like everyone else, they have had their problems, disappointments, and joys. Most have had experiences they later regretted and confronted personal decisions as difficult to make as a decision about adoption.

Many social workers are dedicated and competent. Some are not. Most will have some prejudices, hopefully within their awareness. If you feel your social worker is treating you unfairly or is not competent, you should discuss this with the social worker and his or her supervisor.

Services to Birthparents

Ellen, a twenty-three-year-old college student, is four months pregnant. She was referred to Mrs. Reynolds at Bundle of Joy by a local birth control clinic after she decided

to continue her pregnancy. Ellen supports herself with her
earnings from a part-time job and some assistance from her
parents, who live in another part of the state. She met Jim,
the father of her child, while on vacation in another state.
Ellen still has made no decision about a plan for her child.
Jim is not yet aware she is pregnant.

Ellen does not know what to expect from the adoption agency
or from Mrs. Reynolds, her social worker. Generally adoption
agencies provide birthparents with the following services:

- counseling
- assistance in planning for the practical aspects of whatever
  plan the birthparents choose
- assistance in planning and preparing for the child's adoption
- legal services relating to the surrender and adoption of the
  child
- counseling and record keeping after the adoption

Costs

Adoption agencies usually provide services to birthparents
without charge. Birthparents are responsible for the costs of
pregnancy, childbirth, and their child's maintenance before the
agency assumes responsibility. Sometimes private medical insurance or welfare (AFDC) can help defray these costs.

Counseling

Usually adoption agencies provide counseling to assist you in
deciding on a plan for your child. To talk to a counselor you do not
need to have already decided to place your child for adoption.
Your social worker should discuss all of the alternatives and help
you consider each in the context of your own values and your actual situation.

Even if you have already made your decision, the social worker
will want to talk about the various choices with you. Adoption professionals realize how serious and permanent this decision is.
They want to be sure that you understand the implications of your
decision and that the decision is right for you and your child.

Generally, counseling extends beyond just a discussion of the
alternatives. Most birthparents find themselves confronting the
issues of their own values, their sexuality, their pattern of relationships, and their personal goals.

Ellen, described above, discussed the choices with Mrs. Reynolds and found herself wondering why she had decided against having an abortion. Why had she gotten pregnant? How did she feel about Jim, her child's father? Did she really want to finish college? In the process she developed a much clearer idea of the way her life was going and what her goals were.

Several weeks before her child was due Ellen decided on adoption. Following her decision, Mrs. Reynolds kept in close contact, helping with the practical arrangements and providing her with emotional support.

Birthparents who are relinquishing their children for adoption can see their children after birth, name them, and present them with a gift or letter if they wish to. Many birthparents find seeing their child reassures them that the child is healthy. Often their decision to place the child for adoption becomes firmer. Their child is no longer an extension of their own bodies but has become a real person who needs what the adoptive parents can give.

Ellen named her daughter Anne, gave her a small gift, and wrote her a letter explaining why she had placed her for adoption. Mrs. Reynolds will see that the gift and the letter are forwarded to the adoptive parents.

Birthparents often experience the loss of a child through adoption as they would the loss of a child through death. As part of the natural mourning process they feel anger and sadness. This was the case for Ellen. Mrs. Reynolds helped Ellen talk about these feelings, reassured her that this was a normal reaction, and encouraged her to get beyond her loss.

Jim, the father, was informed of Ellen's plan and consented to the adoption. Had he lived in the area, counseling services would have been available to him too. Fathers usually participate in planning for their children and sometimes experience the same confusion, difficulty in making a decision, and feelings of loss that birthmothers have.

An unplanned pregnancy and a decision about the child is often a family problem. Since many young birthparents are dependent on their families, the latter often contact an agency. When they do, family counseling is provided.

Assistance in Planning

Ellen decided on adoption. However, had she decided differently, Mrs. Reynolds would have directed her to resources that would have assisted her in her other plan.

Mrs. Reynolds helped Ellen arrange a number of practical matters relating to pregnancy, childbirth, and life after delivery.

Together they worked out a plan for Ellen's medical treatment. When a mother does not have a private physician, adoption agencies usually arrange for the use of the agency's doctor and hospital. If a mother does not have medical insurance or sufficient financial resources for the childbirth, the agency may find other ways to meet her medical costs.

During the last months of pregnancy mothers are often unable to work. The social worker and the birthparent(s) can develop a plan for this contingency — perhaps living with family, the assistance of AFDC, or a maternity home.

Equally important will be Ellen's plans after the child is adopted. Sometimes in making a decision about adoption, birthparents decide to make other major changes in their lives, such as to move, end a relationship, or change careers. While it will be Ellen's responsibility to act on these decisions, her social worker can help her examine their implications and their practicality.

Planning for the Adoption

An adoption involves much more than the legal transfer of a child. Preparing for the adoption of a child also involves making specific arrangements, gathering information, evaluation, and other paper work. Before the agency will accept your child it will most likely:

- evaluate your child
- explain its procedures for transferring a child
- take a medical and social history of the birthparents
- find out the birthparents' preference for adoptive placement
- find out the birthparents' feelings about future meetings with their child

Evaluation of the Child

Agencies require that a child be evaluated medically. Depending on the child, the agency may want to evaluate the child further. (See Chapter Three, The Child.) Agencies do not accept every child for adoption. For example, if your child is born severely retarded an agency may not accept responsibility for him or her. Some problems that may delay or prevent adoption are:

- The child has uncertain or severe medical problems.

- The agency has difficulty or is unable to legally free the child for adoption.
- No adoptive parents are willing to take the child.

Agency Procedures

Agencies generally have routine procedures for adoption arrangements. These procedures may need to be adjusted to individual situations and preferences. Generally, if a child is newborn, the agency will take the child from the hospital and place him or her for several weeks to several months in a temporary foster home. The agency evaluates the child during this time, and the birthparents can reconsider their decision to place for adoption. Normally the child would then be placed in an adoptive home. These procedures vary, depending on the agency and the individual child and birthparents.

The agency will also explain the birthparents' legal rights and responsibilities, the legal procedure for adoptions, and the legal implications of adoptions.

Histories

The agency will want a complete medical and social history of each birthparent. Your medical history will be important to your child throughout his or her life. Many physical and emotional conditions have a hereditary basis and are prevalent in certain families. If heart disease is frequent in your family, your child will need to know this in order to take precautions as an adult. You will not be around to communicate this information to your child or a physician.

Your social history is your life story — a description of your background, family, physical characteristics, interests, talents, religion, personality, current situation, and why and how you made the decision to place you child for adoption. This information will help the agency match your child with a compatible adoptive family. Also adopted children, as they grow up, will be curious about their birthparents and what they have inherited from their birthparents, and will certainly want to know why they were adopted. Knowing about you will be important to your child's development.

Relevant and necessary information will be presented to your child's adoptive parents. The entire record will be kept in the adoption agency's confidential files. Later your child or the adoptive parents may want to reconsult the agency to refresh their memories or to consider the information from a different perspective. (The child's use of the background information is explained in Chapters Nine and Eleven.)

This information is confidential. Only nonidentifiable information about you will be presented to your child or the adoptive parents. Ellen, mentioned before, will be described as a twenty-three-year-old college student — not as Ellen O'Neil, twenty-three, a student at Friendly Mountain College.

Your Preference in the Choice of Adoptive Parents

Agencies, when possible, place children in accordance with the wishes of their birthparents. For example, you may wish your child to be placed with Jewish parents who have other children. However, agencies will seldom delay for long a child's placement or place a child with less satisfactory adoptive parents in order to follow the preferences of the birthparents.

Some agencies, particularly if your child is a white infant, will present you with nonidentifiable descriptions of several appropriate adoptive families and allow you to choose the adoptive parents.

Future Meetings with Your Child

Under normal circumstances, neither the court nor the adoption agency will give birthparents and adoptees identifiable information about each other or arrange for meetings between them.

Increasingly, adult adoptees are attempting to locate and meet with their birthparents. (See Chapter Eleven, The Adult Adoptee.) The law may currently or in the future make provisions for meetings and exchange of information between your adult adopted child and yourself. Many agencies now warn birthparents about this possibility and record in their files the birthparents' feelings about such a meeting.

Legal Services

Adoption agencies provide the legal services necessary to free a child for adoption. The parental rights of both parents must be terminated in order for a child to be free for adoption. (Refer to Chapter Four for an in-depth treatment.) This happens in the following ways:

- death of the parent
- consent of the parent
- without the parent's consent, under court order

Generally in agency adoptions both the birthparents consent to the adoption. In some states, California for example, the parents can relinquish or surrender their child to an adoption agency for adoptive placement. This does not require a court hearing and permanently severs the legal relationship between birthparent and child. Other states require that the birthparents appear in court and, in the presence of a judge, consent to their child's adoption. Agencies and courts are reluctant to accept the parents' consent immediately after a child is born.

Sometimes the termination of one or both of the parents' rights cannot be obtained through their consent. This can happen, for example, if the parent's identity is unknown, if the parent is incompetent to give his or her consent, or if the parent is unwilling to consent to adoption. In all cases where the consent of a parent cannot be obtained, a court order freeing the child for adoption is needed.

These situations can be extremely complicated and can delay a child's adoption. One of the more common problems is that the child's father is unknown or cannot be located. Many mothers are reluctant to identify the father. *Failing to give the father's name almost always delays a child's adoption and may, if the father later objects, result in the adoption being set aside.*

Services to Children

Anne, the daughter whom Ellen and Jim relinquished to the Bundle of Joy Adoption Agency is now one month old. At three days old she was transferred from the hospital to the Hazel foster home, where she will remain until her adoptive placement. After her first demanding scream it seemed likely that Anne would grow into a healthy, noisy infant. However, the agency was cautious. Now both Mrs. Hazel, the experienced foster mother, and the agency doctor believe that Anne is normal and ready for adoptive placement.

Anne can be placed quickly and easily. Older or handicapped children require more extensive service from the agency. However, for all children in their care most agencies provide these services:

- legally free a child for adoption

- supervise, maintain, and counsel a child before the adoptive placement (see Chapter Three)
- evaluate the child medically, psychologically, developmentally, and educationally, if appropriate (see Chapter Three)
- assist the child in parting from the former relationship (see Chapter Three)
- find the child an appropriate adoptive family
- provide the child with supervision and support until the adoption is final (see Chapter Eight)
- reassume responsibility for the child if the placement fails before the adoption is final
- postadoptive counseling and record keeping (see Chapter Eleven)

Agencies, for good reasons, generally evaluate and screen a child before accepting a parent's relinquishment or consent to adoption. Once it accepts a child for adoption, the agency is responsible — like a parent — for providing the child's support, supervision, medical care, living arrangements, and emotional and physical welfare. Agencies, of course, plan to pass these responsibilities on to adoptive parents.

Most agencies will accept for adoption even a very hard-to-place child if the agency believes adoption is necessary for the child's welfare. Such children may need considerable counseling, maintenance, and medical treatment to prepare them for adoption.

Some children, free and prepared for adoption, are not easily placed in adoptive homes. For these children agencies try to recruit adoptive parents. Occasionally finding families for these children is beyond the agency's ability, and various agencies within a region will pool their resources. Bundle of Joy, for example, will send a description of one of their children to other agencies. Another agency may respond by sending Bundle of Joy the names of qualified adoptive parents who might be interested in the child. If Bundle of Joy is unsuccessful in this attempt, it may widen its search and perhaps list the child with one of the national adoption agencies, such as AASK or ARENA. On rare occasions the agency will not be able to find adoptive parents and will be responsible for the child until he or she is an adult.

The placing agency supervises children once they enter their adoptive homes until the adoption is final — usually six months to a year. Sometimes the adoptive placement fails during the adjustment period. This can occur for a variety of reasons — the child develops an unforeseen medical condition, the adoptive parents divorce, or the agency recognizes a major problem in the family and cannot recommend that the adoption become final. The adoption agency then again becomes responsible for the child and will try to find other adoptive parents.

Services to Adoptive Parents

While Ellen and Jim are deciding to place their little Anne for adoption, Jerry and Mary Mann, would-be adoptive parents, are being contacted by the Bundle of Joy Adoption Agency. More than two years ago the Manns called Bundle of Joy, among other agencies, indicating that they wanted to adopt an infant. The agency told them they would have to wait and wait they did. Now a social worker, the ubiquitous Mrs. Reynolds, invites the Manns to an orientation meeting for prospective adoptive parents. For Jerry and Mary Mann the process is beginning.

Finding a Child

When the Manns decided to adopt a child, they wondered whether there would ever be a child for them. Some of the ways to increase your chances of adopting a child are:

- being flexible in choosing children (see Chapter Three)
- adopting independently (see Chapter Six)
- contacting and applying at many agencies

Both the Manns considered requesting an older or hard-to-place child but honestly decided they wanted to adopt an infant. They also decided they wanted the security of an agency adoption.

Contacting Agencies

Agencies should be contacted by phone, letter, or in person. Indicate your wish to adopt a child. Specify whether you are interested in adopting an older child or a child with special needs. This may give you priority over other applicants. Ask what the agency's general requirements for adoptive parents are. Some agencies, for example, will not place children with single parents. Inquire about their fees. Have the agency outline their procedures. They may place your name on an inquiry list or send you an application. Whatever their system, be sure that they have noted your request in writing. Then check in with the agency every few months and let them know you are still interested.

Fees

Public agencies usually do not charge a fee. Private agencies are funded by donations and the fees they charge adoptive parents.

The fees of private agencies run from nothing to over $3,000 and are usually based to some extent on family income. These fees help defray the overall costs of services to birthparents, children, and adoptive parents. But most agencies will not reject a promising and financially secure adoptive parent because of the inability to pay a fee.

Each agency has its own fee system. A common practice is to charge a minimal registration fee, perhaps ten dollars, a larger amount when the agency is ready to begin an in-depth evaluation, and the remainder at intervals until the adoption is final. Even if you do not adopt a child you will probably pay some portion of the fee.

In addition to fees charged by the agency, you will probably be responsible for some legal costs. The agency should meet the cost of freeing the child for adoption. Adoptive parents usually pay the cost of the adoption, generally from $250 to $500. Public agencies will often meet the legal costs for low or moderate-income families.

The Homestudy

A homestudy is a written report on your fitness as potential adoptive parents. The report is based on a combination of written documentation and a social worker's evaluation after a number of face-to-face interviews.

You may be close to obtaining your child when the agency begins your homestudy. This is a costly, time-consuming process that agencies are reluctant to begin unless they feel the possibility of placing a child with you is good. A homestudy usually requires two months to complete.

Written Documentation. Agencies ask that you furnish or complete a variety of documents, such as:

- birth certificates for parents, children, and other family members in the household
- marriage certificate

- divorce decrees
- W-2 or income tax return from the previous year
- bank, savings, and credit union statements
- insurance policies
- statement of your holdings in property and stocks
- statements of outstanding loans
- naturalization or visa papers
- doctor's report from current medical examination
- reference from your employer
- two to six other references
- a completed application

Many agencies require that these documents be evaluated before the social study can begin.

☑ Warning: Omitting documents or falsifing an application could result in your child's adoption later being set aside. (See Chapter Four, The Legal Process.)

Social study. Agencies usually have general procedures for the interviews between you and the social worker. Typically a couple is interviewed jointly, each spouse interviewed separately, and the entire family — other children included — is interviewed together in their home. There may be several more joint or separate interviews depending on agency procedures and the needs of the family.

With reason, most families are apprehensive when the interviews begin. They correctly assume they will need a favorable evaluation in order to get a child.

Your social worker will not expect you to be a storybook family. Social workers know that sometimes your dishes will be dirty and your kids will be rude. They know that you will be anxious about the interviews. Social workers will be much more concerned with how you get along and what you can offer a child. Some of their major concerns will be:

- your motivation for adopting a child
- how a child will fit into your home and your lifestyle
- the strength of your marital relationship, if you are married
- how you resolve problems
- how you handle stress
- what kind of child you want and why

Social workers usually want to help would-be adoptive parents become parents — not to disqualify them.

Jerry and Mary Mann are waiting for Mrs. Reynolds, the
social worker, to come to their home for her first visit. Both
of them have taken the day off work for the occasion. Mary
has given the house its best cleaning since her mother last
visited. They both now sit nervously waiting for Mrs.
Reynolds' arrival. Mary worries that a previous, short marriage will make it impossible to adopt. Jerry knows that he is
usually quiet with strangers and wonders what Mrs.
Reynolds will think. He lights up a cigarette. Maybe she disapproves of smoking.

When Mrs. Reyonlds actually arrives, the Manns' apprehension diminishes. She seems a fairly normal, likeable person. Their
conversation is informal, not the policelike investigation they had
expected. She asks why they want to adopt, what their goals and
their backgrounds are.

Mrs. Reynolds has already noted on the application that Mary
has been married before. She asks Mary about this marriage, why
it broke up, and why she thinks her marriage to Jerry is different.

Jerry, she notices, is quiet. Is this because he is a quiet person,
distant, or perhaps not as interested in adoption as his wife? This
is only the first interview. Mrs. Reynolds will keep this concern in
mind for later interviews. By the third interview her question is
answered, when she needs to cut Jerry's conversation short to get
to another appointment.

You, like the Manns, probably have something very special to
offer a child. If you relax and are yourself your social worker will
be more able to appreciate this.

Now that we have told you you must relax, here are some things
you should do while you are relaxing (good luck):

- Be honest with the social worker.
- If you are confused or have a question, ask for clarification.
- Do not try to present yourself as perfect.
- If you have doubts, use the social worker to help you work
  them out.
- If you disagree with something the social worker says, say
  so and explain why.

Results of the homestudy. Your social worker should give you a
good idea of how he or she views you as adoptive parents during
the course of the interviews. you can ask questions if you are in
doubt as to the conclusions. Following the homestudy you will be
informed of the general recommendation, but you probably will
not receive a copy of your evaluation.

A favorable recommendation after the homestudy means that you can now be considered for a child under the agency's care. It does not mean that you will get a child. An available child must need the type of home you can provide before he or she will be offered to you. However, your acceptance will qualify you to register with adoption pools (special needs children) and participate in some intercountry adoption programs. (See Chapter Seven, Intercountry Adoptions.)

Problems with the homestudy. Your social worker should tell you if he or she believes you would have problems becoming adoptive parents. The difficulties will be pointed out to you, and perhaps some action on your part to improve your chances will be suggested, such as involving yourself in counseling or postponing adoption. You can also ask that the social worker's recommendations be reviewed by a supervisor.

Consider carefully the agency's reasons for rejecting you. If you feel that their reasons will not affect your ability to be a good parent, you can apply at another agency or perhaps contest the agency's decision.

Matching the Child with the Adoptive Family

> Little Anne is ready for adoptive placement. The Bundle of Joy professional staff, including Mrs. Reynolds, her supervisor, other social workers, and the agency director, Mrs. Gror, gather together to match Anne with adoptive parents. Anne's birthmother, Ellen, has requested that Anne be placed with a Catholic married couple. She suggests the Manns, feeling they will meet the birthmother's requests and Anne's needs. The Manns, themselves indicated a preference for a daughter. Another social worker suggests two other families. After considerable debate the director, Mrs. Gror, decides that the Manns will be offered Anne.

Agencies consider a number of factors in matching a child with adoptive parents. The preferences of the child, birthparents, and adoptive parents are taken into account. Usually an attempt is made to match the adoptive parents' religion, racial background, and educational potential with that of the birthparents. Agencies try to place children with parents who can meet their anticipated needs or who can encourage their special talents. Often adoptive parents are chosen because their physical appearance is similar to the child's.

Currently, agencies are becoming less rigid about matching a child. Agencies now tend to consider the ability of adoptive parents to meet the child's needs more important than matching appearances.

With a healthy newborn like Anne the agency has many choices. Any number of families will be qualified and willing to accept her. The agency will be very selective.

An older or hard-to-place child presents the staff with more challenges. Probably the agency will have only a small group of adoptive families to choose from. And these families will need to be especially qualified to handle the child's adjustment and special problems. The agency will be much more concerned with the abilities and willingness of these would-be parents than with their racial background or appearance.

Bringing the Child and the Adoptive Family Together

> The Manns arrive early one morning at Bundle of Joy. Mrs. Reynolds called them last week and described Anne. Of course they were interested in her. They spent the week buying baby things, calling relatives, and thinking of names. Finally Mrs. Reynolds brings Anne to them. After half an hour together Mrs. Reynolds asks them whether they feel Anne is the child for them. Both the Manns are thoughtful, realizing again what a decision this is. They decide to adopt Anne. The next day they return, receive medical and formula instructions, and leave Bundle of Joy with their daughter, now renamed Sonja.

Before a family and a child make a commitment to each other two things usually occur — an exchange of background information and a meeting or meetings between the prospective parent and child.

Background information. Before the meeting, Bundle of Joy informed the Manns of Sonja's health status, the background and heritage of her birthparents, the situation leading to her adoption, and the agency's guess as to her potential abilities.

With an older child or a child with special needs the situation is more complicated. Prospective adoptive parents are presented with medical and psychological information. This material is checked out with the family's own pediatrician and other local resources. Adoption agencies are required to inform prospective adoptive parents of any major condition or problem that may affect the child's adjustment or development. (See Chapter Three, The Child.)

Often the agency and the family work out a plan to meet the child's special needs. For example, a plan may be developed to provide for securing and paying for a child's speech therapy.

Adoption subsidies. The plan may involve an adoption subsidy. States vary in the benefits offered. Most states will pay medical and some support costs in order to encourage families to adopt hard-to-place children. (Adoption subsidies usually save tax-payers money by removing children from government-supported foster homes and institutions.)

Meetings. Preplacement meetings are arranged in order to allow a child and parents to get acquainted and evaluate each other.

With an infant such as Sonja, the family is reasonably certain they can accept the child before the meeting. The need to adjust to each others' personalities is slight in comparison with an older child. For them, one meeting may be sufficient.

For older children, even those only six months old, one visit is seldom enough. Older children need more contact in order to ease their adjustment. The older the child, generally, the greater the need for preplacement visiting and contact. Both the family and the child need to adjust to each others' personalities, and both need to make a commitment to the adoption. This may involve many visits, both in the office and in the adoptive parents' home, as well as counseling sessions before the family and the child are ready to commit themselves.

What if you do not want to accept a child? Sometimes would-be adoptive parents meet a child and decide the child would not fit in their family. You may be feeling pressured into making a decision before you are ready or you may genuinely feel that this child is not for you. Share your doubts with the agency. This is not the time for you to accept this child. The agency will want to know your reasons. Sometimes a family needs to meet a child in order to realize that his or her needs are beyond their abilities. Your refusal to accept a child will not necessarily bar you from being considered for another.

The Adjustment Period

Between your child's placement in your home and the finalization of the adoption (usually six months to a year), the agency will be assessing your child's adjustment, evaluating your home, and supervising your child's placement.

You will be responsible for your child. However, should you flounder or fail the agency will resume responsibility. The agency will also recommend to the court whether the adoption should be finalized. (Chapter Nine describes the adjustment period in depth.)

Finalizing the Adoption

One year after Sonja joined the Mann's family she, her parents, her family's attorney, Mrs. Reynolds, and Mrs. Gror gather in a judge's chambers. The judge enters. A few questions are asked, recommendations read, and Sonja becomes the child of Jerry and Mary Mann.

If You Believe an Adoption Agency Is Treating You Unfairly

The child is the adoption agency's primary client. An agency chooses adoptive parents according to its perception of a child's needs. The age, sex, marital status, race, religion, and lifestyle of would-be adoptive parents can be considerations.

An agency's judgement of what is best for children in general or one child in particular is obviously subjective. Usually, though, it will conform to the values of the community, the agency's orientation, and social work ethics. However, an agency can be arbitrary and develop requirements that have absolutely no bearing on your ability to be a parent.

It is important to distinguish between public and private adoption agencies. A public adoption agency is required to use criteria in its selection of adoptive parents that relate directly to an applicant's ability to be a parent. Private agencies must abide by their state's licensing requirements and their own standard procedures, but can be more arbitrary in their requirements. For example, an agency can require all adoptive parents to be in good standing with their religious group.

You, a prospective adoptive parent, have no right to adopt a child. You should, however, be treated equally among other applicants. For example, a private agency can require *all* adoptive parents to be married. It cannot require you alone to be married. If you feel an agency has disqualified you by singling you out, fight its decision!

Some of the more common complaints prospective adoptive parents have with agencies are:

- disqualification during the homestudy

- a child is never placed in their home even though a homestudy has qualified them as adoptive parents
- after a child has been placed in their home, the agency does not recommend that the adoption be finalized

Prospective adoptive parents who are disqualified as a result of the homestudy or who have difficulties after a child is placed in their home should have access to the agency grievance procedures and later, perhaps, the courts. It is more difficult to use these means if the agency never places a child in your home.

Most agencies have grievance procedures. These procedures will be described in the agency's manual. (You can ask to see this.) Agencies are required to follow their standard procedures for selecting applicants and for resolving grievances. Public agencies usually have an appeals procedure. Generally private agencies require that you try to resolve your differences through the chain of command, which is often as follows:

- the social worker
- his or her supervisor
- the agency director
- the board of directors
- the state licensing agency

You can go to court *only* after you have exhausted all other means of working out your differences.

The Bundle of Joy Adoption Agency informs carrot-topped Richard Bell that it does not accept redheaded adoptive parents. Studies show that men with red hair abuse their children and have violent tempers. Richard must first control his temper and then follow the agency grievance procedures.

Richard met the agency social worker, her supervisor, the agency director, and the board of directors. He is very tired but still no closer to being a parent. Richard can now engage an attorney and file suit against the agency. Winning the suit, though, would only require Bundle of Joy to consider his application fairly — not to give him a child.

☑ Note: A prospective adoptive parent whose grievance cannot be resolved within the agency procedures will need an attorney.

Six:

Nonagency Adoptions

In General

A *nonagency adoption*, an *independent adoption*, a *private adoption*, or a *direct adoption* is an adoption without the assistance of a licensed adoption agency. These adoptions occur between unrelated adults and children, and between relatives.

In the past, nonagency adoptions were the most common kind of adoption. However, with the nationwide development of adoption services and public assistance programs to help defray the cost of pregnancy and childbirth, nonagency adoptions are now less advantageous for unrelated adults and children.

Generally, we, the authors, believe it is better to use the services of an adoption agency. There are many times, however, when an independent adoption is indicated. For example, you may want your sister and brother-in-law to adopt your child. Perhaps your stepdaughter has actually seemed to be your daughter for years and how you want to adopt her. Or you have raised Andy, a friend's child, and now want to adopt him.

Most nonagency adoptions between nonrelatives are successful. Some studies show little significant difference between the success rate of agency and nonagency adoptions. Usually adoptive parents, whether they adopt through agencies or independently, are well motivated, loving parents. However, we feel adoption is such an important step that the additional legal safeguards, evaluation, and counseling provided by agencies should be used.

Most states continue to provide for independent adoptions between nonrelatives. The rationale for allowing these adoptions is that a child's birthparents should be able to provide for the child's welfare by choosing the adoptive parents.

The current shortage of healthy, white, adoptable infants forces many affluent prospective adoptive parents to consider nonagency adoptions. Many are unwilling to wait the years necessary to adopt through an agency or are unable to meet the often rigid agency requirements. (Agency requirements for adoptive parents are discussed in Chapters Two and Five. Ways of finding adoptable children are described in Chapter Three.)

Unfortunately the lack of adoptable babies has also encouraged the thriving business of black market adoptions — a business in which the adoptive parents pay an intermediary and perhaps a birthparent for a child. This kind of independent adoption is *illegal* in every state.

This chapter discusses the process of nonagency adoption, and its advantages and disadvantages for the birthparents, adoptive parents, and children. Be sure to read Chapter Five, Agency Adoptions.

Independent Adoptions between Nonrelatives

Maryanne Anderson is an unmarried pregnant woman wanting to place her child for adoption. She is referred to an attorney, Mark Hatt. Mr. Hatt has been contacted by the Greens, a childless couple wanting to adopt a baby. He has talked with the Greens and is convinced they will be good parents. Mr. Hatt describes the Greens to Maryanne, and Maryanne's situation to the Greens. Both agree to this adoption. Mr. Hatt arranges for the necessary consents and other legal matters. After Maryanne's son is born the Greens take him home from the hospital. Six months later the adoption becomes final.

Intermediaries

Typically a physician, lawyer, minister, or mutal friend acts as an intermediary or matchmaker by bringing together birthparents who want to place their child for adoption and persons who want to adopt. These intermediaries function somewhat like an adoption agency. They are usually well-intentioned individuals who sincerely do their best for everyone. Ideally, the birthparents' problem is solved, the adoptive parents have their wanted child, and the child has a good home.

However, intermediaries are seldom trained to counsel and to evaluate birthparents, adoptive parents, and children. Birthparents and adoptive parents planning an independent adoption must examine their motivation, make their decision, and evaluate the adoption themselves.

Before the Child Is Placed

As with any adoption, the parental rights of the birthparents must be terminated. In an independent adoption, usually both birthparents voluntarily give their consent for specific people to adopt their child. For example, Maryanne Anderson and Robert Smith consented to the adoption of their son by Alice and Phillip Green. Depending on the state, either written consent or verbal consent in the presence of a judge will be required. (For a detailed discussion, see Chapter Four, the section, "Consent of Persons Involved.")

Often adoptive parents agree to pay some of the birthparents' costs. If this is the case, the birthparents and prospective adoptive parents should be clear as to exactly what and how much these expenses are, and what the consequences will be should either party change their mind about the adoption. Be sure this is a written agreement. (Such agreements are discussed in detail in Chapter Four.)

☑ Reminder: A birthparent who plans to accept money for pregnancy expenses should be very sure of her decision. Although she may have changed her mind, she may feel and be obligated to follow through with the original adoption plan.

Transfer of the Child

It is the birthparents themselves, not the intermediary, who legally make the placement. Some states require a child's birthparent or relative to physically give the child to the adoptive parents. Other states will allow the adoptive parents to pick up a child at a hospital, or at a doctor's or attorney's office.

Investigation of Adoptive Placement

Several states require that an independent adoptive placement be approved by the court or welfare department *before* a child enters an adoptive home.

Generally, the adoptive placement is evaluated *after* the child enters the home of his or her would-be parents. In most states, as part of the process of legally finalizing an adoption, a court representative or delegated agency investigates the adoptive home and makes recommendations to the court. This process is similar, but seldom as thorough, as the hometudy done by an adoption agency. (See Chapter Five, the section, "The Homestudy," and Chapter Eight, the section, "The Social Worker's Visits.")

Interstate Adoptions

In many independent adoptions, the child and the birthparents reside in one state and the adoptive parents reside in another. Adoption laws vary from state to state. Some states *do not accept* the consents and procedures of another state. This can result in delays, difficulty in finalizing an adoption, and additional expense.

Persons considering an interstate adoption should investigate the adoption laws of both states before agreeing to an adoption. Prospective adoptive parents will probably need the services of attorneys in both states.

Finalizing the Adoption

The court will require a child to be free for adoption. The usual number of written documents are required, as well as the results of the court-ordered investigation. Also, the court will demand an accounting of adoption expenses. We definitely suggest that you engage the services of an attorney for these proceedings. (For a thorough discussion of such court proceedings, see Chapter Four, The Legal Process.)

Even though the birthparents have surrendered their child to the adoptive parents, the adoptive parents do not become legally responsible for the child until the adoption is finalized in court. The birthparents may have the right to reclaim the child. The adoptive parents can also decide not to go through with the adoption and avoid becoming permanently responsible for the child. (See Chapter Four for further discussion.)

Gray Market Adoptions

> Maryanne and Robert consent to the Greens' adopting their son. The Greens pay some of the expenses of Maryanne's support during pregnancy, her medical costs, attorney's fees, and adoption costs. The total cost for the Greens is $3,900.

Gray market adoptions are *legal* in most states. In these adoptions neither the birthparents nor the intermediaries profit personally. Adoptive parents pay only the costs. Intermediaries may receive only reasonable fees for their services. Some states will allow only the payment of direct medical and legal costs — not the cost of an intermediary's time spent matching birthparents and adoptive parents.

Birthparents with low incomes are seldom helped by gray market adoptions. Public assistance will usually meet their costs. Moderate-income birthparents may find they need the adoptive parents to help with the cost of pregnancy and childbirth.

☑ Caution: Be sure to comply with the legal requirements of your state regarding the payment of expenses. Failure to do so could result in criminal charges and in the adoption being set aside.

Black Market Adoptions

> The Greens pay Mr. Hatt, their attorney, $10,000 for the adoption of their child. $1,500 is used to pay the birthparents' medical expenses. Another $2,000 is paid directly to the birthparents for "related expenses." The attorney's legal fee is $7,500.

Adoption can be a business — and a very profitable one. Willing adoptive parents have paid up to $35,000 for a healthy, white infant. The birthparents seldom see a large portion of this fee. The intermediary — doctor, lawyer, or just baby broker — pockets most of the profits. The children, of course, are not placed according to their best interests but according to the ability of the adoptive parents to pay.

Many people are aware of the extreme examples of black market adoption — women being paid to become pregnant and deliver babies to waiting adoptive parents, mothers entering hospitals and giving birth to children under the name of the adoptive parent, and baby brokers offering parents thousands of dollars to relinquish their children for adoption.

These situations and any other adoptions for profit are illegal in every state. The birthparents, the adoptive parents, and the intermediaries may all be subject to criminal charges. Worse, perhaps, is that later a child's adoption could be set aside.

Most black market adoptions are not disastrous for the child. The adoptive parents who pay for their children are usually not criminals or unfit parents. They are simply people with the money and desperation to subsidize an illegal and immoral business. They pay for their child with more than just money — with the fear of criminal penalties, of losing their child, and of blackmail.

Independent adoptions are legitimately more expensive than agency adoptions. It is difficult to draw the line between the usually legal gray market adoption and the always illegal black market adoption. Attorneys and doctors do need to be compensated for their time spent counseling birth and adoptive parents and arranging an adoption. However, the "sale" of a child is often disguised in unreasonably large legal, medical, or pregnancy-related expenses.

How Much Should an Adoption Cost?

You can be more confident that an independent adoption is legitimate by insisting on an itemized statement of cost.

The legal costs for a simple adoption to which both birthparents consent should not be more than $1,000. The cost of an attorney's time arranging the adoption may be additional. Unless there are complications in delivery, the medical costs related to childbirth should not be more than $2,500.

Be suspicious if an adoption costs more than $5,000 to $6,000. If the adoption costs more than $10,000, you can generally assume that it is a black market adoption.

Should You Participate in a Nonagency Adoption?

Again, we feel that agency adoptions are usually better for the child, birthparents, and adoptive parents. This is, of course, only our opinion. We will present the pros and cons as objectively as possible. You must make your own decision.

Possible Advantages of Agency Adoptions

- A licensed adoption agency will operate according to the law.
- The birthparents, adoptive parents, and child are all clients; services will be provided to them all.
- The birthparents, adoptive parents, and child are all thoroughly evaluated by trained professionals before a child is placed in an adoptive home.
- There is more variety in the choice of child or adoptive parents.
- More background information is available.
- The security of knowing that adoption procedures are correct and legal exists.
- They are less expensive for the adoptive parents.
- When difficulties occur in a placement, an agency will act as a back-up resource.
- The confidentiality of all parties is usually better protected.

- During the period between placement and finalization children are usually more free from any attempt by the birthparents to reclaim them.
- Records are maintained and may be accessible years later if needed.

Possible Advantages of Independent Adoptions

For the child:

- Many independent adoptions allow an infant to be placed directly from the hospital into an adoptive home. Most agency placements require a wait of two weeks to several months in a temporary foster home.
- The placement may have been selected by the birthparents.

For the birthparents:

- The costs of pregnancy and childbirth may be paid.
- Evaluation and counseling by an agency will not be necessary.
- The birthparent may be able to choose the adoptive parents.
- If the birthparent changes her mind before finalization, it is usually easier to reclaim the child.

For the adoptive parents:

- The adoptive parents are generally the primary client.
- The waiting period for a child may be shorter.
- The requirements for being adoptive parents may be less stringent.
- This may be the only way to adopt a newborn, healthy, white child.
- Evaluation and counseling by an agency will not be necessary.
- The adoptive parents may be able to evaluate and have personal contact with the birthparents.

Points to Remember

- Use only the services of a reputable intermediary.
- Talk with your *own* attorney before you agree to any adoption.
- Always have a child's health evaluated before making an agreement about adoption.
- Be sure the parental rights of each birthparent are termi-

nated, either by consent or by court order, before you take a child into your home.

- Question any arrangement that is too easy.

Family Adoptions

Neither of baby Ellen's young, unmarried birthparents are prepared to assume the responsibilities of raising her. Ellen's paternal grandparents, Mrs. and Mrs. Ortiz, wish to keep her in the family and adopt her. Both birthparents consent.

Nonagency adoptions between blood relatives are legal in all states. When the relatives are able to show that they would make reasonably good parents and both birthparents consent, these adoptions are usually straightforward and accepted by the courts. (See generally Chapter Four, The Legal Process.)

The emotional aspects of family adoptions are discussed in Chapter One, the section, "The Family of One Parent Cares for Your Child."

Stepparent Adoptions

Sidney Cohen, the father of Laurie, nine, and Lisa, seven, died years ago. Their mother, Betty, later married Bill Wishard. Bill, with Betty's consent, asks the court to become the adoptive father of Laurie and Lisa.

This example is the authors' own adoption twenty-one years ago. For us as well as for most people involved in stepparent adoptions, such procedures are simple, readily accepted by the courts, and inexpensive.

A stepparent adoption is the adoption of your husband's or wife's child. In some states, such as California, the legal requirements and procedures for stepparent adoptions are different from those for other adoptions. These differences make stepparent adoptions easier to obtain.

In our adoption, the consent of the father was not needed. Documentation of his death and the consent of the mother were sufficient. But usually a child's other birthparent is living. His or her consent may be required for the adoption, although some states make the consent of the noncustodial birthparent unnecessary. For example, California allows stepparent adoptions without the consent of the noncustodial parent if he or she has not supported or visited the child in a year. In other states, custody orders can specify that consent for adoption is not necessary. (See Chapter Four, The Legal Process.)

Many stepparents, for all purposes except those of the law, are a child's parent. They support the child, and have known, raised, and cared for the child for years. In these situations, a stepparent adoption will recognize and protect the reality of a present family situation. These adoptions are also often advantageous for the birthparents, who lose their parental rights and are therefore no longer obligated to support or be responsible for the child.

Some of the problems of other adoptions are avoided in stepparent adoptions. Children are not detached from their biological roots. Their backgrounds are accessible. They are usually able to make contact as adults with their birthparents if they wish.

While stepparent adoptions are easy to obtain they are just as binding as any other adoption. Many stepparents have adopted children, later divorced their spouses, and been ordered to support *their* children. Be sure that you really want all the responsibilities of being a parent if you are planning a stepparent adoption.

Seven:

Intercountry Adoptions

In General

Intercountry adoptions, foreign adoptions, and *international adoptions* are adoptions that occur between a parent or parents of one nationality and a child of another. In the situations described here, the parents will be residents and citizens of the United States and the child a resident and citizen of another country.

These adoptions are arranged in three ways. Some are arranged through an adoption agency based in a foreign country. Others are set up by a domestic agency that has foreign contacts. The procedures for both varieties of agency adoptions are similar. Finally, some adoptions are arranged independently. These adoptions are somewhat similar to domestic nonagency adoptions and often use the services of an intermediary. (Nonagency adoptions are discussed in detail in Chapter Four.)

Intercountry adoptions are generally more difficult and risky than adoptions within the United States. These children may need to be legally adopted in both their country and the U.S. Immigration and naturalization procedures must be followed. Often the child is adopted unseen and unknown by the adoptive parents. When these children finally join their adoptive families, they must adjust not only to a new family but also to a very different culture.

In many ways, however, a foreign adoption is similar to any other adoption. (See Chapter Two for a general discussion of the factors to consider in deciding to become an adoptive parent, and Chapter Three for a discussion of the needs and backgrounds of adoptable children.) This chapter describes the specific emotional, legal, and practical aspects of making a foreign child your own.

Why Adopt a Child from a Foreign Country?

Deborah and Ron Simms, a married couple in their mid-thirties, found themselves unable to have birthchildren.

Both wanted a family and the experience of raising an infant. They investigated the usual agencies, even independent adoptions, and finally were discouraged. Both wanted to have a baby in their home before they were much older. Deborah, who had studied Asian history in college, thought about adopting a foreign child.

The Simms, like many families, thought of adopting a foreign child when they discovered the realities of adopting a child in the United States. They wanted a healthy, young child and did not want to wait years.

They investigated foreign adoption further, and looked closely at themselves and the way they lived. Deborah had always been interested in Asian culture. Gradually the Simms became more and more excited about adopting an Asian child. Both found themselves feeling that an Asian child would provide them with the joy and experience of being parents and that the child's background would add to their lives.

Many families consider intercountry adoption but decide that this type of adoption is not practical for them. Some reasons *not* to adopt a foreign child are:

- You do not want to contend with the extra red tape of a foreign adoption.
- You feel the risks of adopting a foreign child are too great.
- You want to adopt a foreign child primarily to save the child from horrible living conditions.
- You are unable to accept a child who may be racially and ethnically different from yourself.
- You feel your family or community would be unwilling to accept a "different" child.

Any adopted child needs to be a first choice for his adoptive parents. Do not turn to intercountry adoption only because you feel no other children are available to you. Other children *are* available. You may need to wait or accept an older or hard-to-place child. Many adoption professionals, in fact, discourage foreign adoptions. They feel that the United States now has too many of its own children in need of adoptive placements.

Agency Adoptions

The Simms researched foreign adoptions and decided they wanted to adopt a Korean child through an adoption agency. Deborah and Ron wrote many agencies and after examining the replies decided to work with two of them. These agencies

asked the Simms to complete an application and to arrange
for a homestudy to be done by a local agency, Bundle of Joy
Adoption Agency. After they completed the applications,
the Simms waited almost a year. Then the local agency contacted them. One of the foreign agencies, New Tomorrow,
was offering them a year-old-boy, Kim Pang Pak.

Preliminaries

Before the Simms actually decided to adopt a foreign child they
did their homework. First they contacted their state agency responsible for adoptions. (These are listed in the appendix of this
book.) The states vary in their policies and regulations concerning
foreign adoptions. It is advisable to check with the agency in the
beginning. Some would-be parents and children do *not* meet the
requirements for the children's adoption or easy entry into the
United States.

The Simms also talked with local adoption agencies. Generally
a local agency does the homestudy that is required for a foreign
agency placement. But some local agencies will not do these
homestudies. Others may not work with certain adoption agencies. Be sure to check on agency procedures in your area. A local
agency is also often a good source of information about other
agencies and may be able to tell a prospective parent which are
the best agencies to use.

Finally the Simms wrote to various agencies specializing in
foreign adoptions. They asked about procedures, requirements,
and the types of children available. From the material returned
and the information provided by the local agencies, the Simms
selected their two agencies. (The names and addresses of international adoption agencies can be found in the appendix of this book
and are also available from your local state agency responsible for
adoptions.)

Application, Homestudy, and Learning about the Child

The Simms completed the applications provided by both agencies. The application itself was very similar to those used by
domestic agencies. The Simms informed each agency that they
were working with the other.

A homestudy, an in-depth evaluation of your fitness as adoptive
parents, will be required. (See Chapter Five, the section, "The
Homestudy.") Some families find themselves in the adoption
agencies' version of "Catch 22." The local agency may not be will-

ing to do a homestudy until the would-be parents are accepted by an intercountry program. The intercountry program will not accept them until an agency has done a homestudy. When this happens, have one agency write the other indicating that you are being considered for their program.

Eventually the Simms were contacted by a social worker from Bundle of Joy, the local adoption agency. New Tomorrow, the foreign agency, had forwarded a description of the child and a photograph. Some families are contacted directly or through their attorney. The social worker discussed the child with the Simms before they accepted him. Had the Simms decided not to accept him and had good reasons, they might have been put back on the waiting list for another child.

Immediately following their decision to accept the child, the Simms contacted the U.S. Immigration and Naturalization Service in order to arrange for the child's entry visa.

The Child

> Kim Pang Pak is a year-old Korean boy whose birthfather is unknown and birthmother is deceased. He was brought to the New Tomorrow Orphanage after his mother died. Pak is a healthy, normal child who was born with a noticeable birthmark on his right cheek. Eventually, with the medical techniques available in the U.S., the birthmark should almost vanish.

Korea, like many other developing countries, has tightened its requirements for intercountry adoptions. Children are to be placed first within their own country if possible. Thereafter foreign parents may be considered. Pak was offered to the Simms after a year's wait, and then only because his birthmark could easily be corrected by techniques available in the U.S.

Meeting the Child

> A bewildered little Pak boarded a plane for the flight from Korea to the United States. He and four other soon-to-be adopted children were accompanied on the flight by the wives of two U.S. servicemen. Waiting for them were the Simms and four other anxious couples. When the children finally arrived the Simms saw a different and much older child than they remembered from his photograph. The boy, now called James Pak, greeted his strange looking father and mother with a yawn.

The Simms, like many adopting families, did not need to go to their child's country to adopt him. New Tomorrow arranged for James Pak's transportation and escort. The Simms shared the cost of the escort's airfare with two other sets of adoptive parents. Sometimes these flight plans do not go smoothly. Flights are delayed and canceled. Occasionally parents will go to meet their child only to find that a last minute health problem has postponed their child's arrival.

On the advice of New Tomorrow, the Simms had James examined by a pediatrician the day after his arrival. Even children who have been medically evaluated by agencies can arrive with parasites and other medical problems. Aside from a minor cold, the doctor found James Pak very healthy.

Nonagency Adoptions

Norman and Marilyn Cole are the parents of two teenage daughters. Norman is employed as a consulting engineer for an American construction firm. His most recent job assignment took him monthly to a remote construction site in Colombia, where he supervised the construction of a large water project. Norman, missing his own family, befriended some of the young boys also "supervising" the construction, particularly nine-year-old Juan Rodriquez. Norman grew to expect Juan's presence in the back of his jeep, and finally asked about Juan's family. Both Juan's parents were dead. He was being raised by his aunt along with five cousins in a one-room house. Norman began bringing Juan presents, food, and vitamins. Then after discussing Juan with his wife and daughters, Norman approached Juan's aunt. He asked for permission to adopt Juan. She and Juan agreed.

The Coles contacted their state agency handling foreign adoptions, asked about procedures, and arranged to have a homestudy done. Marilyn flew to Colombia, and she and Norman legally adopted Juan there. They used the assistance of the U.S. consular staff and a Colombian attorney the consulate recommended. They then arranged for a passport, an exit visa, and the U.S. entrance visa necessary to bring their son, still a Colombian citizen, to the United States.

In many nonagency foreign adoptions, the would-be parents do not have an existing relationship with the child. These adoptions are very similar to independent adoptions in the United States. An attorney, doctor, director of an orphanage or hospital, or interested citizen is often the intermediary who brings the children and parents together. This is usually the rule for Latin American adoptions. Generally these adoptions require the services of an attorney in the foreign country and in the United States. Very often adoptive parents will need to go to the child's country, adopt the child, and personally bring the child back home.

Foreign independent adoptions have all the risks and possibilities for exploitation of domestic independent adoptions. In fact, as the adoptive parents are likely to be unfamiliar with the country's culture and language, the risks may be greater. (See Chapter Six: Nonagency Adoptions.)

Some of the ways to avoid the worst pitfalls in foreign nonagency adoptions are:

- Have your child evaluated medically by your own doctor before you agree to adopt. The U.S. consular staff can recommend a reputable local doctor.
- Check the reputation of your intermediary with the consular staff.
- Inquire about your intermediary with other parents who have used his or her services.
- Have the U.S. consular staff, if possible, assist you with every step of the process in the foreign country.

Procedures for Legal Adoption

Adoption procedures are different in every country. They vary here from state to state. In a foreign country your adoption agency or the U.S. consular staff will advise you. In the United States your own adoption agency, your state agency responsible for adoptions, your attorney, or all three should advise you concerning the procedures for legal adoption.

In Foreign Countries

You will need to adopt your child at least once, maybe twice. Some countries require that children be adopted before they leave the country. This can be accomplished by one or both parents actually being present during the adoption proceedings or, in many countries, by proxy adoption. In *proxy adoptions* the would-be parents give their power of attorney to a person in a foreign country who represents them and adopts a child for them. Proxy adoptions may be acceptable in another country but are not sufficient here.

In the United States

Children adopted by proxy adoption must be adopted again in the United States. Some children are allowed to leave their countries without formal legal proceedings. It may even be necessary to begin adoption proceedings here before the child enters the country. This may help the child secure a preferential visa. (See below.) Adoption in the United States is usually not required for children adopted according to formal adoption proceedings in their own country when the adoptive parents were present. However, adoption here may provide a child with additional legal safeguards and may help him or her secure a more favorable visa.

Immigration

Before a child leaves a foreign country, the child must have a passport from that country and usually an exit visa. An adoption agency or the U.S. consular staff should help you obtain these.

The U.S. Immigration and Naturalization Service requires that an adopted or to-be-adopted child be examined by a doctor from the U.S. Public Health Service before the child enters the country. Adoption agencies usually arrange for this.

In the United States

The adoption of a child by an American citizen does not alone entitle the child to enter the United States or to automatically become an American citizen. Both require application and the meeting of requirements.

Most foreign adoptees enter the U.S. on an I-600 visa. This is a preferential resident visa that exempts a child from the usual quotas and waiting periods. Adopting parents need to obtain the U.S. Immigration and Naturalization Service's I-600 form, "Petition to Classify an Orphan as an Immediate Relative," provide a number of requested documents, and pay a thirty-five dollar nonrefundable fee.

The requirements for the I-600 visa were changed substantially in October, 1978. Children will now be eligible for the visa if the conditions outlined below are met.

The adopting parents:

- are a married couple or over twenty-five years of age if single persons
- are U.S. citizens (at least one of them, if a couple)

- have certified to the Immigration and Naturalization Service (INS) that the preadoption requirements of the state of residence have been met
- are able to give assurance that proper care for the child will be provided

The child is:

- an orphan or half-orphan whose surviving parent is unable to provide adequate care
- under the age of fourteen
- irrevocably released in writing for emmigration to and adoption in the United States

The more important changes in the requirements of the I-600 visa are the inclusion of single adoptive parents and the provision for *mandatory* investigation of the adoptive parents' home and their fitness as parents. Previously, this was not required for the I-600 visa and was done only at the discretion of the state of residence or of the facilitating adoption agency.

Generally this visa is used for two groups of children. In the first are children coming to the United States to be adopted. James Pak, the child of the Simms, is an example. Most often these are agency adoptions. The adoptive parents work with their own adoption agency and their state agency regulating international adoptions. The child can then be certified by the agencies as meeting the preadoption requirements of the state of residence.

In the second group are those children who have been seen by their adopting parents before the completion of an adoption abroad. Juan Cole, Norman and Marilyn Cole's child, is such a child. The adoptive parents must have a completed homestudy and should notify their state agency and the INS at least six months prior to attempting to adopt the child abroad. These parents should be prepared to spend enough time in the foreign country to complete their child's adoption. The U.S. visa will not be issued until the adoption is complete.

A child who is ineligible for an I-600 visa, for example one fourteen or older still may be able to enter the United States and become a resident. The adoptive parents may need to live abroad with their child for some time, arrange for a special act of Congress to provide them with a visa, or apply for a medical or student visa.

☑ Reminder: The Immigration and Naturalization Service requires that parents register their alien children each January.

Naturalization

Naturalization is the process by which one becomes an American citizen. Any child adopted after the enactment of the October, 1978 laws and eligible for an I-600 visa is now *immediately* able to apply for U.S. citizenship. Children adopted before that date or who enter on another visa still must wait two years before applying for U.S. citizenship.

Costs

Usually intercountry adoptions will not cost substantially more than a domestic adoption. International adoption agencies charge fees comparable to those charged by agencies placing American children. Costs can run between $1,500 and $3,000. The expenses of airfare for the child and the escort or adoptive parents may be additional. Some adoptive parents pay for the child's support before his or her arrival in the United States. Attorney's fees here usually cost an additional $300 to $500.

The costs of independent foreign adoptions are more variable. The adoptive parent may need to travel to a foreign country, engage an attorney and intermediary, and perhaps maintain the child for a period of time.

Special Concerns in Adopting a Foreign Child

Adoption, for any child and parents, requires considerable adjustment. Children need to find a place for themselves within their new families and the families must alter their lives to accommodate the children. (For a more detailed discussion of adjustment see Chapter Three, the sections, "Older Children" and "The Minority or Racially Mixed Child," and Chapters Eight and Nine.)

Foreign children and their new families adjust to much more. Parents who adopt through agencies usually receive a briefing on the child's culture, what to expect from the child, and advice on easing the strain of the adjustment period. Families who adopt independently may find some of the same services available through the agency that investigates their home, a local adoption agency, or the local Welfare Department or Department of Social Services.

James Pak, the Simms' adopted Korean one-year-old, arrived tired and confused. On his second day in America the Simms discovered him cranky, withdrawn, sniffling, and only picking at his food. In the past day he had survived a long flight, new people, and a totally new culture. The Simms had been prepared for James' reaction to the changes, but they were so excited they found it a little hard to accept. Several weeks later, though, James seemed to find a comfortable place for himself within the family.

Juan Rodriquez Cole found his new world much more difficult. He left a rural village in Colombia, was adopted in a big city by his new father and mother, flew to the United States, and then was greeted at a big city airport by two sisters smiling through their braces. Both were excited and talking in a language he could not understand.

Once in their home he found the new world even stranger. Juan knew his way around his old home, but here he felt he knew nothing. The food was strange, his new family ate their food in a different way, and he had toys he did not even know how to use. After a month at home Norman went back to Colombia to work, and Juan was left with all these strange women he could not understand. He missed his aunt and his cousins. Somehow he had not expected things to be like this.

The Coles, too, found Juan difficult to understand. Norman noticed that Juan had lost much of his usual self-assurance and cockiness. Juan was like his shadow. Marilyn was shocked when she discovered his table manners and that he did not know how a flush toilet worked. She found herself learning the fine art of pantomine. The girls, though, seemed to have the easiest time understanding and being with Juan.

The Coles, and other families adopting older foreign children tried to help their child adjust to a radically different world by:

- learning a few words and phrases in the child's language
- speaking softly, slowly, and simply to the new child
- avoiding company and confusion
- delaying enrolling the child in school
- not insisting that the child learn everything immediately

Eventually Juan did find a place for himself in the Cole family. Within a year his English was fluent and, to his father's regret, he had forgotten some Spanish. He was placed two grades behind in school. The school plans to promote him several grades when he catches up with his classmates. Juan found a best friend. Together he and his friend terrorize the neighborhood with their much too fast bike riding.

The Simms, the parents of James Pak, and the Coles, the parents of Juan, are now concerned that their sons may become too assimilated. Both families want their sons to be at ease both at home and in American culture. But they do not want their children to lose touch entirely with their own cultures and countries. They try to keep their children's heritage alive within their families. The Simms and the Coles plan some day to take their families to visit their sons' native countries.

Availability of Children

In most intercountry adoptions the child comes from an underdeveloped country, usually in Asia or Latin America. Generally these countries are reluctant to have their children adopted abroad. Many countries consider children a national resource, as valuable to the country as its oil, timber, or agricultural land. Exporting children for adoption also brings with it an admission that a country does not have the means to care for its own children.

Generally countries stop allowing large-scale export adoptions when their economies become more affluent and they begin to develop domestic services for their children. As a result the availability of a given country's children for foreign adoption changes. In the 1950's most foreign adoptions by Americans were from Europe. Then Asia, predominantly Korea, Vietnam, and the Philippines, became the primary sources of international adoptions. These countries have now stopped or limited international adoptions. Korea, for example, now has a quota for the foreign adoption of healthy young children, and prefers that foreigners adopt older children, handicapped children, or groups of brothers and sisters. Currently, it appears that new possibilities for adoptions are opening up in some Latin American countries and India.

The adoption agencies have had their greatest success in Asian countries. Latin American countries seem to view large-scale agency adoptions with suspicion. This is probably the result of a lack of understanding of what adoption really means in the United States, fear that the children will be exploited, and some traditional hostility toward "The Colossus of the North." Most adoptions in Latin America are independent adoptions.

Adoption trends change rapidly. The information presented in this chapter is general and may soon become outdated. Be sure to check with your state agency regulating foreign adoptions and individual adoption agencies for current information.

Part III
Creating the New Family Tree

Eight:
The Adjustment Period

In General

Your long-awaited child is now in your arms. You decided to adopt a child, endured a long wait, perhaps worked with an adoption agency, and now you are a parent. A movie version of your story requires you now to fade happily and slowly into the sunset. However, your story is really just beginning.

You and your child are now embarking on the most important part of the adoption story — the emotional process of becoming a family. *Closeness will not come immediately or just because you and your child wish it.* Time and shared experiences will make you a family.

Keep your expectations reasonable. Your newly adopted six-year-old daughter may not immediately want to be hugged or instinctively know that in your family vegetables, as well as hamburgers, are to be eaten. Expecting your child to love you or know your family's rules immediately will only leave you feeling frustrated and a failure.

You are, of course, delighted to finally have your child. However, do not expect yourself to feel love right away for this young stranger who has joined your household. You will need time to develop a bond with your youngster.

Adjustment works in two ways. Your child will need to develop a pattern of behavior that fits in your family. And you will need to adjust to the child's personality, the demands of a young person, and to being a new parent or the parent of an additional child.

Discussed in this chapter is the practical and emotional process of becoming a family, specifically during the time between a child's placement in the adoptive home and the finalizing of the adoption.

(The concerns of the adoptive family after the adjustment period are described in Chapter Nine, The Adoptive Family through the Years. Adoptees as adults and their search for their biological roots are discussed in detail in Chapter Eleven.)

Preparing for Your Child's Arrival

Birthparents have nine months' warning of a child's arrival. Changes during pregnancy are unmistakable evidence that a child is really coming. During this time expectant parents can prepare themselves emotionally to be parents, anticipate changes in their lifestyle, and make practical arrangements for having a child in their household.

Adoptive parents usually wait more than the natural nine months for their child. The waiting period is so long that the reality of actually being a parent often fades. Then suddenly, with a telephone call, the child's arrival becomes imminent — perhaps only a week away. The suddenness of a child's arrival and the logistics of arranging all the practical aspects of becoming a parent leave many new adoptive parents excited, as well as tired and frazzled.

Employment

After an adoptive placement, one parent usually needs to quit or take a leave from his or her job. Some agencies require that one parent stay home with a child until the adoption is final. Even if this is not required, it is advisable to cut back on outside responsibilities while you and your child adjust to each other.

You may plan to have day-care provided by someone other than yourself. However, your adopted child first needs to develop an attachment to you before he or she will feel safe with a babysitter. Many employers who provide pregnancy leaves will also provide adoption leaves.

Clothing, Bedrooms, Toys

Infants come to their adoptive parents with perhaps the clothes on their back, a bottle of formula, and a toy. Some agencies even require that children be changed into clothes provided by the adoptive parents before they are taken home. You will need to purchase just about everything.

Older children usually come with some clothing and toys. You will want to prepare some things for your child's arrival. Depending on the child's age it may be important to child-proof your home, removing poisons and fragile or dangerous items from reach. Be sure your child has a space that is his or her own — a bed, a bureau, a closet — but do not arrange everything. Your child will probably want to participate in decorating the room and selecting new clothes.

Santa should come at Christmas — not when your child enters your home. A few gifts will excite and occupy the child, but too many will be overwhelming. You want your child to appreciate your love and affection, not just your material gifts.

Insurance

You will want to alter your insurance policies, especially any medical insurance policy, to include your new child. Not every policy will allow the inclusion of a child prior to the finalization of an adoption.

Pediatrician

Before your child arrives, select a pediatrician. The agency or the child's previous doctor will give you a medical history of your child. See that the pediatrician gets the history and, if possible, examines it before you take your child home.

Bringing Your Child Home

Three days ago Bill and Juanita Russell brought home their new four-month-old son, Daniel. The couple had begun looking for a child to adopt three-and-a-half years ago. Just two weeks ago the Russells were alerted that the adoption agency might have a son for them. These last weeks have been exciting and frantic. Between purchasing clothing and a crib, arranging for a diaper service, and calling relatives, both Russells were exhausted when Danny finally arrived. Juanita had arranged for six months' leave from her job. Neither Juanita or Bill were aware what a change in routine an infant brings. Both wish they could be really sure what his cries mean.

For a discussion of the needs and background of the adopted child, see Chapter Three, The Child.)

Infants and Young Children

Even an infant like Danny is aware that his surroundings have changed. Probably he is somewhat distressed by the change in caretakers and homes he is experiencing. He may cry frequently and perhaps not eat as regularly as before. This reaction should diminish in several days to a week.

Bill and Juanita want him to become comfortable in their home and with them as quickly as possible. As with any new child, the Russells try to limit visiting and confusion. It was impossible to keep the delighted grandparents away, but the Russells are cutting back on mass visiting. They will invite friends over in a few weeks.

Older Children

Older children join their adoptive families in a much more gradual fashion — generally, the older the child the more gradual the transition. Families who have adopted through agencies will have had a number of preplacement visits with their child. Even if you adopt independently try to visit your child several times before you bring him or her home. Visits will ease the transition and give you and your child a better opportunity to evaluate each other.

Most older children entering an adoptive home will be on their best behavior. Their manners may be excellent, they may say nice things about you, and they may like everything you like. In short, they are not relaxed or sure enough of you to be totally themselves.

You will probably be tense yourself. You want your child to like you and to feel at home in your home. Probably you are on your best behavior too. When your six-year-old accidently breaks a dish, you stop yourself from reacting the way you ordinarily would.

Expect yourself and your family to feel the strain. Your child is still a stranger in your house. Neither the child nor you are totally at ease in each other's presence. With your wife or husband or one of your other children you feel comfortable talking, but with this new child you probably just do not know exactly what to say or do.

Many families try to ease the strain by doing special things with their child. Save these for later when your family will enjoy them more. Try to help your child find his or her place within the everyday structure of your household. Some regular chores, involvement in family recreation, and an introduction to the neighborhood children will probably help.

You and your child will need some time apart. Give your child a physical space to be alone in if the child wishes it. Older adopted children need to know that they do not need to be with their parents all the time. You will certainly need some time away from your child — alone or with your spouse. Let your child know that there are some times when you want to be alone.

After the Newness Has Worn Off

Infants and Young Children

After several months, Juanita and Bill Russell, the new parents mentioned in the above example, find that some of the excitement of being new parents has left. Both are tired. Juanita feels she is always occupied with Danny but never really busy. She misses her friends at work. Bill feels that he and Juanita are just not getting enough time together. Every time they begin a conversation Danny needs attention. Both the Russells have found that a child does not only add something to your life — a child demands that you give something up too. Unfortunately, adoptive parents have not been exempted from this reality.

Under the day-to-day demands of being a parent, you may miss the freedom you had before. Many birthparents feel exactly the same way. Your life is now very different and you realize it. After several months, most parents accept the changes, taking the joys with the drawbacks.

This day-to-day care you provide your child will make you a family. As your routine and the child's become interwoven a bond between you develops. There is nothing magical about this process. It is simply the way any parent and child — birth or adoptive — develop an attachment.

Older Children

Eight-year-old Tommy was so good when he first joined your family. He kept his room clean, thanked you properly, and delighted in helping you with the yard work. Now, two months later, this model child has turned into a terror. His room is a disaster. He hates liver, and when you tell him to eat it anyway he screams a well-known explitive.

Tommy is not a budding juvenile delinquent, and you are not failures as parents. Tommy is secure enough now to test you — to see if you can handle his worst behavior and to see if you really intend to keep him.

You have changed too. Tommy is no longer a stranger to you. While initially you might have allowed his room to be a mess, now you expect him to conform to the rules of your house. You realize that Tommy is not your whole life. You want to spend some time alone with your spouse and your friends.

With an older child you will need to be accepting and also able to set firm limits on behavior. Do not be afraid to say "No." Tommy needs to be told that some words are not appropriate dinner conversation for an eight-year-old. Tommy will interpret your failure to do this as your not caring or your being unable to control him. He needs to learn that you can and you will discipline him when he misbehaves, and that even with his misbehavior you are still committed to him.

This is an important lesson for you as parents, too. Unfortunately, good relationships do not materialize without work. Along with living together and closeness comes some amount of conflict. You will become close through your good times together and also through working out your conflicts.

Eventually Tommy will retreat from showing you his worst. But he will not be that model and probably very frightened youngster who first entered your home. His personality, interests, and preferences were developed before he came to you. He cannot and should not change totally to please you.

As with any older adopted child he has less than a storybook background. He lost his birthfamily and this loss will color his relationship with you. More than another child, he will need to see if you really intend to keep him.

Many families adopting an older child use the assistance of a professional counselor. A counselor can help your family clarify the problems you are experiencing, get a perspective on your situation, and provide your child with support and an opportunity to grow.

Brothers and Sisters

Many adopted children entering a family find they have instant brothers and sisters. If you have adopted your newest child through an agency, your older children were probably included in some way in the process. Your children will have been interviewed by the social worker during the homestudy and may have been included in the preplacement meetings. Adoption is a family process. You may be getting a son, but your other child will be getting a brother.

Families who adopted independently should make their other children aware of a coming brother or sister and, if possible, allow their other children to meet the new child before he or she enters the home.

Initially your other children will probably be excited about their new brother or sister. Children are usually ice-breakers. They will accept the reality of the new child and will quickly lose any self-conciousness about being on their best behavior. You may need to control their enthusiasm, perhaps telling your four-year-old that she cannot drag her new brother to every house on the block.

Your children will soon realize that your family is now different. They may not like the difference. This new child demands more of your time and they get less of it. A new child is the center of attention, fussed over by you, grandparents, and relatives.

It makes no difference that this new child is adopted. Most children will, at times, resent new birth as well as adoptive siblings. Your other children may become enraged and tell you to take the new baby back to the agency. They may become more cranky, babyish, and demanding. They may fear that you will like the new child better than them. These are normal responses. Your other children will need your time and reassurance that you love them and that they are still important to you.

Relatives

Before you bring your child home you will probably have discussed with relatives your decision to adopt, your experiences in finding a child, and some details of the new child. By now you have a good guess how your relatives will accept your child.

Most relatives will share your excitement and delight. But unfortunately some may never accept your child, however much you and your child wish it. For some people, a biological tie is more important than an emotional attachment or the child as a person.

Remember that you are adopting your child — not your parents or your brother. If your parents refuse to accept your adopted child as their grandchild, they are the losers. You may, however, still want to continue having some sort of relationship with a relative who does not accept your child. Adoptive children and birth-children can survive having one relative who irrationally dislikes or disapproves of them. However, it is important that adopted children are not constantly in the company of a disapproving person and that they realize the disapproval is not their fault.

You may find that your family's attitude changes when they actually meet your child and accept the reality of your commitment. It is possible that your aunt, in spite of her very worst intentions, may become a doting relative.

Friends

Yours is an interesting story, and for many people your new life is full of mystery and drama. Lots of people have children by birth, but adoption, even though common, is still a curiosity. Your friends will be interested in your motivation, in the adoption process, and in your child's background.

You can be straightforward with your friends and acquaintances, telling them that your child is adopted and something about the adoption process.

You may neither want nor need to tell them everything. Some of your friends' questions — perhaps, "Why couldn't you and your husband have your own child?" — will be insensitive and not really their business. You no more need to answer this question than one about your health, finances, or sex life. However, you may be comfortable answering this kind of question or feel that answering is easier than explaining the reasons for your refusal.

You should handle carefully questions about your child's background. Revealing some aspects of your child's background may be disturbing to some people and cause them to label your child. More importantly, you want to be the one to tell your child about his or her background, not a neighbor or a playmate.

After several months your friends' curiosity will usually diminish. You will become just another family and your child will be just another kid on the block.

The Social Worker's Visits

Whether your child came to you through an adoption agency or by independent placement your home probably will be investigated prior to the legal finalization of the adoption.

With an independent adoption, a representative of the court, a social worker or perhaps a probation officer, will investigate you and the placement. This investigation is very similar to the homestudy performed by adoption agencies, which is discussed in detail in Chapter Five, the section, "The Homestudy."

Your situation may be different from that of parents who adopted through agencies. You are beginning your evaluation *after* your child is in your home. The social worker may ask you to provide some written documentation, such as financial and health statements. Your social worker will probably interview you and your family several times in your home.

From the written material and the interviews, the social worker will prepare a report and recommendations for the court. In the adoption proceedings the judge will consider the recommendations and then decide whether the adoption will be finalized. (See Chapter Four, The Legal Process.)

Families who adopt their child through an agency are usually evaluated by the same placing agency. An exception occurs when the adoptive parents live outside the area serviced by the original agency. Then, the court-required investigation is conducted in a similar manner to that of an independent adoption.

In agency adoptions the evaluation of your home and your child has been made before placement. The agency will continue their relationship with you and help you make the placement work for you and your child. For families with older children the adjustment is almost always stressful. Your social worker can be a support for your family and a link for your child during the transition period.

Even if you have adopted an infant, expect the social worker to visit you three or four times before preparing a report and recommendations for the court. The main concern will be your progress in becoming a functioning family.

What If the Adoptive Placement Is Not Working?

You made a commitment to try to become a parent to a child when the child entered your home. You are *not* legally bound by this commitment until the adoption is finalized in court. However, once it is final you are like any other parent. You are responsible for your child until adulthood — in sickness or in health, in juvenile hall or in church. (See Chapter Four for a complete discussion of the finality of adoption decrees.)

If you still have doubts about wanting to be a parent or about your child's adjustment in your home, voice your concerns *now*.

Those parents who received their child through an agency will have a back-up resource. The agency can help them clarify the problem and may be able to help them work out a solution. For example, you may discover that the infant placed with you has a severe hearing loss. The agency can help arrange for an adoption subsidy and a treatment program. With this help you may be willing to commit yourself to the child. Perhaps you may still find that caring for this child is beyond your willingness and abilities, and return the child to the agency. Or you may ask that the legal adoption be postponed until you are sure of your decision.

Families who adopt independently have fewer resources should a placement fail. Sometimes they are able to return responsibility for the child to the birthparents. More often the court and the taxpayers assume responsibility for this child who is now genuinely without a parent.

Failed adoptions are sad and unfortunate. But sometimes, in spite of everyone's hopes and good intentions, a placement just does not work out. It is best then for everyone — parents, child, and agency — to admit the mistake. You will not help the child or yourself by continuing in an impossible situation.

Occasionally an agency or a natural parent must or is willing to reassume responsibility for a child after adoption. (The circumstances in which an agency or a natural parent is obligated to take responsibility for a child are described in Chapter Four.)

An agency may allow the adoptive parents to surrender a child back to the agency. This will occur only if the agency believes it is best for the child. In effect, the adoptive parents surrender their child to the agency for care and eventual placement in another adoptive home, as the birthparents originally did.

Nine:

The Adoptive Family through the Years

In General

The Cohens are a couple in their late forties. Lisa is the director of a medical lab and Jay, her husband, is an insurance salesman. They are the adoptive parents of Steve, seventeen, and Leslie, fifteen. Leslie, adopted as a baby, was the first addition to their family. Three years later Steve, then five, joined them.

The Cohens adopted Leslie and Steve a long time ago. Photographs of the stiffly posed Cohen family immediately after the childrens' adoptions — along with pictures of the Cohens' own wedding, their defunct fish business, Leslie with her pet lamb, and Steve displaying his first track ribbon — fill an old album. The adoptions are now like other important experiences, part of the family history and each family member's identity.

Every family has their own story — their hopes, their common problems and joys, and their individual and family changes through the years. Additionally, a family has the usual concerns of living together and raising children to maturity. But the adoptive family finds some special concerns and challenges. This chapter discusses in what ways the adoptive family is much like any other family and in what ways it is different.

An Adoptive Family Is Like Any Other Family

When Steve was adopted the Cohen family had a thriving fish market. It was a family business with Lisa and Jay working together and later even Leslie and Steve taking their turns after school. Four years ago the business failed, and the family went through bankruptcy and the painful process of facing failure and many changes in their own lives. The Cohens lacked money and jobs, and even felt that their mar-

riage was shaky. Lisa and Jay eventually found new and separate jobs. Steve discovered sports, and Leslie found new
friends and interests. The pain of that time is past, and the
Cohen family can now joke about the business and tell their
fish stories.

The Cohens, like other families, have had times when they felt
very close and times when they felt very separate. The Cohens'
sense of family is the result of their shared experiences — their
togetherness, their joys, the personal and family disappointments, and their problems and solutions.

All families have problems. Sometimes a problem concerns
only one member of the family and at other times the functioning
family as a whole. Recently, for example, Lisa was told that her
lack of a college degree would prevent her from advancing further
in her career. On the other hand, the family's business failure affected them all so that they became, for a while, four individuals
rather than a group. Nevertheless, any change or problem a family experiences affects the functioning of the family group and, as a
result, each family member.

Also, no family stays the same. Even families who are spared an
upheaval like the Cohens' change in some ways. Adults find that
their responsibilities, abilities, and interests are different. Children come to a family, expand their worlds and abilities, and
leave.

Every family member is an individual with his or her own
changing needs. Jay and Lisa are responsible and loving parents.
They are also husband and wife, competent employees, concerned members of their community, and people with their own
personal interests and values. Healthy children, too, have their
individual personalities, abilities, and experiences. As they grow
older, these become more separate from those of their parents.

An Adoptive Family Is Different from Other Families

The Cohens are different from other families. The family as a
unit and as four individuals has had different experiences and
concerns from those of their neighbors. (See Chapter Two, The
Adoptive Parents.)

Different Experiences

They have experienced the process of adoption. Years ago Jay
and Lisa decided to adopt, contacted an agency, were inter-

viewed, waited eagerly for their children, and finally adopted their two.

Steve remembers his life before his adoption — his two foster homes, the social worker talking to him about adoption, meeting his parents, and the court proceedings. Five years of his life were not shared with the Cohens. (For further discussion of the adoption of an older child, see Chapter Three, The Child.)

Usually, in the process of adopting a child, parents discover some special insights into their own behavior, their goals, and their motivation for being parents. Often they come away with a positive attitude toward counseling services and more than the usual willingness to seek counseling when they confront another decision or problem. The Cohens turned to a family counselor when their business and marriage faltered.

Genetic Differences

The dark-haired Cohens look as though they could be related by birth. This, however, is only the result of fortunate agency matching and of chance.

Physical appearance is only one of the minor differences between adopted children and their parents. Lisa and Jay, both people with two left feet, found themselves the parents of an active and athletic Steve. Their favorite sports are music and dinnertime conversation. His energy and love of sports amaze them. Both are proud of his abilities but really have to stretch themselves in order to encourage Steve to pursue his talents.

Jay is quite a talented musician, playing the piano whenever he gets a free moment. Leslie, "Daddy's girl," has persistently tried to learn to play the piano, guitar, and violin. She tries, but just is not very good. This has been a real disappointment to her and to her father, who imagined himself playing duets with his daughter.

The Cohens realized that more than most families they are very distinct individuals with separate interests and talents. They can share their lives, affection, and values, and appreciate and encourage each others' talents, but they cannot share the same abilities and interests.

Identity Concerns

The Cohens adopted their children after they discovered that they were unable to have birthchildren. Both had been brought

up to believe and had accepted that having and raising a family
was part of being an adult. Finding that their lives would not conform to the standard pattern was a shock.

Lisa, particularly, felt a failure. She could not be the mother
she planned or present her own parents with a grandchild. With
time, both the Cohens accepted their loss and adopted Steve and
Leslie.

Leslie and Steve were never second-choice children for the
Cohens. But even years later they still feel some sensitivity and
loss over their inability to have birthchildren. Lisa, in spite of her
best intentions, is jealous and uneasy when other members of
their family talk of expected children.

Normal healthy teenagers are preparing to separate from their
families. An inevitable result of being a successful parent is that
your children will assert their independence and differences from
you.

Like all children, Steve and Leslie Cohen want to find an identity of their own, not just as grown Cohen children. Part of their
differentness will be their birth heritage. They know that they
share experiences, values, and closeness with their adoptive parents. But where did Leslie get her infectious laugh and Steve his
ability to run?

Many teenage and adult adoptees find it critical to consider and
perhaps search out their birth heritage in order to define themselves as separate individuals. Some even need to meet their
birthparents. Adoptees generally do this because of a personal
need — *not* because their adoptive parents have failed them. (See
Chapter Eleven, The Adult Adoptee, for a description of the
adoptee's search for identity.)

Doubts

At times all parents are prone to wondering about their ability
and desire to be parents. Many adoptive parents feel a particular
responsibility to be good parents. Their child's birthparents and
the court entrusted them with their adopted son or daughter.
They wonder if they are doing the best job possible.

All children have difficulties and misbehave. Adoptive families
often find themselves questioning whether the lack of blood ties is
responsible for a relationship problem.

For example, Leslie Cohen is having a hard time being fifteen.
Nothing her mother does pleases her. It seems her mother is too
strict, does not understand, and dresses in bad taste. Lisa Cohen

knows that many fifteen-year-old girls feel this way about their mothers. Still she wonders if Leslie feels this way because Lisa is only her adoptive mother.

Leslie has many boyfriends. One boyfriend becomes the center of her life and then is quickly replaced by another. Jay and Lisa are concerned that Leslie does not have the maturity to handle all these young men, and have tightened their controls on her. She responds by telling them that they are just afraid she will turn out like her "real" mother. The Cohens are hurt by this and begin to wonder if their fear of Leslie repeating her birthmother's problems makes them overly cautious.

Leslie and Steve frequently talk about being adopted and about their birthparents. This has never been a taboo topic in the household. However, Jay's stomach begins to churn whenever this discussion begins again. Intellectually he appreciates that this is a normal, healthy curiosity of theirs. Still he fears that if his children find their birthparents, he may somehow be less important to them.

Fantasies

> Eight-year-old Johnny, the Cohens' nephew, has been sent to his room by his parents after constantly interrupting their conversation. Johnny thinks this is totally unjust. Real parents would never be so unfair. Maybe his real mother is a movie star and has just left him with these people because she is so busy making movies. But someday she'll come and take him away from these unfair people. Johnny is *not* adopted.

Most school-age children have fantasies about being adopted. They imagine a larger-than-life real parent who will rescue them from their horrible predicament.

An adopted child will be able to fantasize about a real birthparent. These fantasies are often very similar to any child's. However, because there is some reality basis to it, the fantasy may linger and be very frightening.

At seven years old Leslie Cohen imagined her birthmother to be a very rich, beautiful woman who would someday drive up in a big car and reclaim her. When she was mad with her parents she hoped for this to happen. At other times she feared that she might be taken away. Her adoptive parents reassured her that all children have fantasies, but that she was their child and would live with them until she was grown up.

Giving Adoptees Information About Their Backgrounds

Adoption agencies generally give adoptive parents information about their child's background. The amount of information received will vary. Little is known about the background of some adopted children. In the past, agencies generally gave less information than they now do. (Background information is also discussed in Chapters Five and Eleven.)

When the Cohens adopted their children they received the information given below.

> Leslie: Her birthmother was an intelligent, unmarried college student. She was Jewish, and her family had immigrated from Central Europe in the 1920's. Leslie's maternal grandfather was a businessman. Leslie's birthfather was twenty-three, a Protestant, and also a college student.

> Steven: His birthparents were a married couple. For unknown reasons, when Steve was two years old their marriage broke up and he was placed in a foster home. His birthparents made no further contact with him. Subsequently, he lived in two different foster homes before being adopted by the Cohens. The Cohens received detailed information about his last foster home.

Before either of the children were placed, the adoption agency discussed their backgrounds with the Cohens. The agency wanted to be sure the Cohens would accept their childrens' backgrounds and be able to present the background information to the children.

Should Adopted Children Be Told They Are Adopted?

Yes. Whether their parents tell them or not, adopted children will probably find out they are adopted. Your relatives, friends, neighbors, or your child's playmates sometimes will slip and tell the child. You do not want to live in fear of someone else's careless remark.

You adopted your child for positive reasons. Obviously adoption is nothing your child or you should be ashamed of. When you tell your child he or she is adopted, you can communicate your feelings and your commitment to your child.

Children who find out they are adopted late and from someone else will be shocked. They may wonder if they can trust their parents at all. They may wonder who they really are, why the information was concealed, and if they should be ashamed of their adoption.

What to Tell a Young Child

The subject of your child's adoption, like your values and feelings about your family, is a part of your normal life and conversation. You will not need to take your two-year-old aside and explain the facts of adoption. Talk about adoption briefly, and as a part of your everyday conversation.

From the beginning, you want your child to be aware of his or her adoption, to hear the word and not think it strange. Do not overuse the word, though. Your child is first and foremost your child — not your adopted child.

Before the age of three or four, your child will probably be unable to really understand what adoption means. At this age children become interested in birth and their origins.

> The Cohens had frequently mentioned Leslie's adoption in her presence. When she was three and they were adopting Steve, she came to her mother with the proverbial question, "Where do babies come from?" Lisa Cohen chose to explain that babies are made by mothers and fathers and grow inside a mother. When another mother and father raise a child, that is called adoption.

Young children will not be interested in knowing everything about their adoption. Their questions will let you know when they are ready for more information. Three-year-old Leslie could not possibly have understood the dilemma of her unmarried birthmother.

What to Tell a School-age Child

School-age children have a marvelous ability to see the blacks and whites of life. There are the good guys and the villains. Birthparents and adoptive parents can magically flit from either category into the other.

You will want to present the child's birthparents in a positive manner. There is no one more judgmental than an eight-year-old, who will probably think being unmarried and having a child is a very bad thing. (Most birthparents placing their children for adoption are unmarried.) Your child probably thinks that smoking, drinking, fudging on taxes, and being too lazy to go to church are also very bad things.

It is important that the birthparents are not thought of as bad people by your child. In most cases birthparents lovingly choose adoption in order to give a child a better future. Children will naturally identify with their birthparents. If the birthparents are presented as responsible, loving people, the children will feel better about themselves.

However, *do not lie* to your child. The backgrounds of some children are unknown. The backgrounds of other children may have some disturbing aspects. You may choose to present some details of your child's background later.

At school age, your child will understand the mechanics of adoption an the practical reasons for his adoption. Those gray areas, the subtleties of the birthparents' dilemma and your decision to adopt, will need to wait until the child is older.

Explain to your child something about heredity — for example, the abilities and appearance inherited by the child from the birthparents. Explain, though, that it is not possible to inherit their mistakes or experiences.

Your child will need to be reassured of the permanence of your commitment. This is an age of fantasies and of thinking that a wish alone can make something happen. Children may feel they were given up because something was wrong with them or fear that their birthparents will return and take them away.

What to Tell a Teenager

Children's ability to handle information about their background and put this information into a perspective will change rapidly during the teenage years. Eventually, as an adult, your child should have *all* the information you have. This information is necessary in order to provide for medical treatment and because the birth heritage of the child is an important part of his or her individual identity.

Most parents find this to be the most difficult time to talk about their child's adoption. Young people need to know about themselves, and this need often becomes interwoven with a normal teenage rebelliousness and desire for independence. Their minds tend to dwell on the subtleties of motivation and social situations rather than just on the facts.

> Leslie Cohen knows everything her parents know about her birth heritage and her adoption. Still this is not enough for her. She is a prober. Leslie wants to know why the Cohens could not have birthchildren and if they are satisfied with

her. She wants to know much, much more about her birth-parents. Is there something horrible in her background no one is telling her? Did her birthparents like animals the way she does? Did they have her sense of humor?

Steve, too, possesses all the meager information available concerning his birthparents and his adoption. He finds the gap in his life story puzzling and disturbing. Why did his birthparents abandon him? Or are they dead? Was he responsible for the break-up of their marriage? Steve's adoptive parents know of his doubts and fears. They wish they could describe Steve's birthparents as loving and caring. All Jay and Lisa can tell him is that they really do not know or understand. Both worry when he speaks of searching for his birthparents. Maybe he will find something he cannot handle.

You will probably not be able to satisfy all your child's questions. You and your child may want to revisit your adoption agency or attorney and try to find out more information. An adoption agency may reveal more of the record than they were willing to do at the time of the adoption.

At this time children may begin to think of searching for their birthparents. Their interest in their heritage is very normal for adopted children, *not* a rejection of their adoptive parents. Teenagers who have a healthy, strong relationship with their parents will probably want their advice and support in learning about and making sense of their birth heritage. (This is further discussed in Chapter Eleven.)

Ten:

The Birthparents through the Years

In General

Vicky Flood, a sixteen-year-old high school student, decided that adoption was the best choice for her and her newborn daughter. Her daughter's father was also a high school student and even less able than she to care for a child. Vicky's own parents remained disappointed and angry. Continuing to live at home would be difficult for Vicky alone but impossible with a child.

Vicky's decision is now made. Her child is in the arms of adoptive parents. Vicky, though, will remember her pregnancy, her daughter's birth, her own painful decision, and her hopes for her daughter's future. She, like other birthparents, will go on with her own life, learn, work, marry, and raise a family.

The story of birthparents does not end with the adoption of their child. They continue to remember their experience and their child. This chapter describes the birthparents' physical and emotional parting from their child and the effects of an adoption on birthparents' lives. (For further discussion see Chapter One, "The Birthparents.")

Parting with the Child

When her daughter was a week old, Vicky visited her for the last time. Her daughter seemed such a tiny and delicate little person. Vicky held her child and explained to the uncomprehending infant the reasons for the adoption. Then this tearful teenager, dutifully advised of her parental rights and the implications of her decision, signed the consent for her daughter's adoption.

Vicky was hesitant to see her daughter after her birth. She feared that by seeing the child she would change her mind. Feelings of affection and tenderness did come. But her daughter became more real to her.

She had made her decision mostly on the basis of her own needs. When she met her daughter, she decided adoption was best for her child's needs too. Vicky was sadder but much surer of her decision.

Meeting with their child gives birthparents the opportunity to be more certain of their own decisions. It also allows them to make their goodbyes, and to be clear with themselves that this episode in their lives is ended.

In the days after she surrendered her daughter Vicky felt lost. For the last nine months her pregnancy and then her real daughter had occupied her thoughts. She missed this child and thought constantly about her.

Her pregnancy no longer stopped her from being the same sixteen-year-old girl she was before. But somehow she just did not feel the same person. Her family and her friends considered her changed. Mostly Vicky felt different herself. She was not interested in her friends' talk of high school boyfriends. Somehow it seemed ridiculous for her parents to continue treating her like a child. Vicky was grieving the loss of her baby, and was also very sure that she herself had changed. But exactly how it would work out for her she did not know.

Birthparents, whatever their age or the age of their child, usually experience emotionally the loss of a child through adoption in a similar way to the loss of child through death. A court appearance, the signing of a consent, or a final meeting brings the emotional reality of the end of a relationship. Then a birthparent experiences an intense grief and feels life is different. With time, this immediate and painful period fades. The birthparent again feels normal, but is still a changed person.

Parting with an Older Child

Andrea Smith is the mother of three children. Andrea is placing the youngest, Jeanne, seven, for adoption. Jeanne is the child of a short-lived relationship with a man now dead. Andrea had wanted an abortion, then adoption, but each time had yielded to family pressure. Finally she tried to raise Jeanne herself. Somehow this didn't work out. Andrea, never able to really love Jeanne, became more and more depressed and sought psychiatric assistance. Finally when

Jeanne herself made a suicide attempt Andrea, with the agreement of her psychiatrist, decided to place Jeanne for adoption.

Parting with an older child is usually difficult for everyone — parent, child, and relatives. Even unhappy and destructive relationships are hard and painful to end. Parents and child both feel the loss and a mixture of guilt, blame, and failure.

It is important to everyone that the relationship be ended clearly, thoughtfully, and definitely. You, unlike the parent of a newborn, have a relationship based on time and common experiences. How you and your child separate will affect both of your feelings about yourselves.

It is not anyone's fault that the relationship is ending. Neither you nor your child are bad people. Sometimes hopes and good intentions just are not enough. Ending a relationship is not the easiest way out. The easiest way would be to ignore a serious problem and do nothing. Adoption is a positive and caring choice.

Parents placing their older children for adoption will usually have the assistance of a social worker or another counselor. Andrea Smith's psychiatrist, Dr. Mary Dell, believed it was important for both Andrea and Jeanne to be clear why the adoption was occurring and understand emotionally that it was permanent.

Dr. Dell brought Andrea and her daughter together one final time. With her assistance they talked over the good times and the troubles the two had shared. Andrea told Jeanne very clearly she would not be able to give her what she needed to be a happy and healthy child. She wanted Jeanne to be adopted by parents who would give her the life she needed and deserved. When they tearfully and sadly parted, they both knew that the relationship was ended and that each would go on with their lives.

Sometime Andrea Smith and Jeanne may meet again. Jeanne will remember her brothers and grandparents. When she is an adult she may try to contact them. She is old enough to remember and have a choice.

(This subject is discussed from a child's perspective in Chapter Three, the section, "Older Children.")

Counseling

Counseling is usually helpful to birthparents parting with their children. It can help you get through the natural process, adjust to the changes in your life, and, equally important, become stronger with the experience.

Occasionally a birthparent will not really accept a decision as final and continue to brood and fantasize about a life with a relinquished child. Some birthparents often do not allow themselves to feel their loss immediately and find themselves still grieving years later. Others are never able to get over the loss of their child. If this is happening to you, professional counseling probably will be helpful. (See Chapter One, the section, "Making the Decision" for counseling resources.)

Through the Years

> Vicky Flood is no longer the same confused and sad young woman who relinquished her child ten years ago. She finished high school, went on to college, and became a teacher. Vicky is now married and expecting a child. She remembers with affection and concern the daughter she relinquished long ago. Is she happy? Did the placement work out?

Vicky, like almost all birthparents, continues to think of her child. Sometimes she wonders whether one of those dark-haired ten-year-olds on the school playground could be her own daughter. At the time of her marriage and then again since she has been pregnant, she has thought of the little red-faced infant.

Now she has decided to try to find out how the placement worked out and returns to the adoption agency to ask for information. Vicky is fortunate. Although she received no identifying information she did discover that her daughter was a healthy, happy schoolgirl. In fact, the adoptive parents were so delighted with her they later added a two-year-old adopted son to their family.

At this time Vicky asked the adoption agency to record her current situation in the adoption records. Her daughter may someday want to consult the records for more information about her adoption. Vicky wants her daughter to know that her birthmother has grown from a confused teenager into a responsible and happy adult. She also wants her daughter to know that then and now she cared.

Currently few states have any mechanism for arranging meetings between birthparents and adult adoptees. However, this may change. Vicky wants her daughter to know that Vicky would like to meet her when she is an adult. She asked the adoption agency to enter this in their records. (See Chapter Eleven for a more detailed discussion of the possibilities for future meetings between birthparents and adult adoptees.)

Part IV

The Search for
the Native Tree

Eleven:
The Adult Adoptee

In General

Most states have enacted confidentiality statutes for adoption records in order to protect the adopted child. The state gives adopted children legal families when their birthparents are unable or unwilling to provide for them. The children are "reborn" into this family, and all traces of their preadoptive past are erased forever. These children are free from whatever stigma might come with their birth heritage, and the adoptive families are free from the interference of the birthfamilies. With a clean slate the adoptive family can develop its own relationships. Additionally, the birthparents are free from their former responsibilities and, perhaps, their past.

These statutes were enacted years ago when "illegitimate" pregnancies were unacceptable and adoptive parents were reluctant to disclose a child's origin or to even disclose that the child was adopted. In these circumstances the permanent concealment of a child's origins was natural and protective. Birthparents, adoptive parents, and the minor child all understood that these records were forever sealed and relied on this being the case.

The best interests of the child are usually the guiding principle for making legal, administrative, and legislative decisions about children. Strict confidentiality of young adoptees' adoption records is probably in their best interest. Generally, the most pressing need of an adopted child at the time of adoption is to form a secure and trusting relationship with the new parents. As discussed earlier, a strong relationship with an adult is believed to give a child a sense of self-worth, a feeling of belonging, and the ability to be competent and intimate as an adult. Confidentiality of adoption records provides for the integrity of the new adoptive relationship by freeing the family from the interference of the birthparents.

Recently, the public has insisted on greater access to personal information available in public records, and adult adoptees specifically are demanding equality with other adults. Many adoptees feel they are being discriminated against because as adults they are denied basic information about their heritage. Other adults are able to secure an original birth certificate, but an adoptee ordinarily cannot.

Proponents of changing the confidentiality requirements point to compelling emotional and medical reasons for allowing adult adoptees access to their records. (These reasons are discussed later in this chapter.) They also argue that the persistence of adoption "myths" delays any change in the law. Among these myths are:

- Adoptees are always children — never mature adults capable of making their own decisions.
- Birthparents remain young, frightened, and confused — not individuals who have grown and changed since the placement of their child.
- Adoptive relationships are fragile — unable to withstand competition with blood ties.

Many adoptees and adoptee organizations are placing increased pressure on the courts, legislatures, and social welfare agencies to change the confidentiality laws and allow adoptees access to their original birth certificates, regardless of their reasons. (The original birth certificates are the most useful tool for adoptees searching for their birthparents. They list the birthparents' names and past addresses.) While no new national legislation or U.S. Supreme Court decision has resulted from this pressure thus far, five states now do provide adult adoptees with their original birth certificate or provide a mechanism for meeting birthparents. Legislation along these lines has been introduced in several states and court cases on this point are pending.

Clearly the trend is toward more open adoption records. Birthparents currently placing their children for adoption and prospective adoptive parents should expect their adult children to have access to their adoption records.

We support allowing adult adoptees access to their original birth certificates regardless of their reasons. But we recognize that this is not a simple issue. On the one hand, the birthparents and adoptive parents were promised confidentiality of the records, and adoptees may be disappointed or perhaps even harmed by discovering their background or meeting a birthparent. On the other hand, adult adoptees, like any competent adults, no longer need protection from their backgrounds or the help of the state in looking out for their best interests. They are entitled to make their own choices and take their own risks.

This chapter discusses adoptees as adults, their need to come to terms with their birth and adoptive heritage, the practical and emotional aspects of searching for their birth heritage, and the current and future status of the confidentiality laws. (See Chapter Four for an in-depth discussion of legal adoption. Chapters Two and Nine also describe the identity concerns of the adoptee. The adoption agencies' implementation of the confidentiality laws is discussed in Chapter Five, and Chapter Ten describes the birth-parents' continued feelings for the adoptee.)

The Adoptee's "Right to Know": The Current Status of the Confidentiality Laws

Adoption procedures and confidentiality requirements are established by each state's legislature, and they vary accordingly. The laws of the states, however, do conform to certain broad federal guidelines and are subject to interpretation by state and federal courts. Often the practical implementation of these laws is decided not by legislation but by an administrative memorandum.

It is important to distinguish between *the right to know* and *the need to know*. Rights are established by law. Only five states — Alabama, Kansas, Minnesota, New Jersey, and South Dakota — allow the adoptees some semblance of a right to know their origins.

Public officials have a duty in most states to conceal an adoptee's origins.

The general trend is for court adoption records, adoption agency records, investigation reports, and original birth certificates to be permanently sealed once an adoption is finalized. (See Chapter Four, The Legal Process. Most states provide for the opening of these records under very special circumstances, which are described in the section of this chapter entitled, "Help with the Search.")

Access to Records

All states, with the exception of South Dakota, provide for a complete sealing of the records until the adoptee is an adult. The great majority of the states permanently deny the adoptee access to the adoption records. (The five states that allow an adult adoptee some access to the records are discussed separately in the section of this chapter entitled, "The Exceptions.")

The records relating to an adoption are usually found:

- in the office of vital statistics, usually within the state or county clerk's office
- in the state agency regulating adoptions
- in the adoption agency that arranged the adoption
- in the files of the attorney for the adoption
- in the court adoption records

Vital Statistics

The agency responsible for vital statistics — birth, marriage, divorce, and death records — usually reissues a child's birth certificate after an adoption. The adoptive parents' names, addresses, ages, and professions usually replace those of the birthparents'. The child generally assumes the last name of the adoptive parents. This new birth certificate then becomes a public record, available to anyone on request.

This occurs either in the normal course of the adoption process or at the specific request of the adopting parents. In some states the adopting parents can also request that the place of birth and the name of the attending physician be deleted from the reissued birth certificate.

The old birth certificate remains sealed in the records. It is available only under court order, or, in Alabama, Kansas, Minnesota, and South Dakota, under some circumstances.

The State Agency Regulating Adoptions

A state agency can acquire adoption records in several ways. Usually, in a relinquishment adoption — an adoption in which the birthparents surrender a child to an adoption agency for adoptive placement — the written relinquishment is filed with the state agency. This same state agency often investigates foreign adoptions.

In nonagency adoptions the court generally designates an agency, often the state agency, to investigate the fitness of the adopting parents and the appropriateness of the adoptive placement. In the course of this investigation information is usually gathered concerning the birthparents, the validity of their consent, and the adoptive parents.

These agencies, in the absence of court orders, keep personally identifiable information about the adoptee's adoption and the birthparents confidential.

The Adoption Agency

An agency often has a wealth of information concerning the adoptee, the birthparents, the adoptive parents, and the reasons for the adoption. This data was gathered as part of the process of thorough preadoptive counseling and evaluation.

In recent years adoption agencies have generally shared much of this information, in nonidentifying form, with the parties to the adoption. Agencies still respect the principle of confidentiality. However, increasingly they recognize the importance of this information to the adoptee's self-concept, the birthparents' feelings of responsibility, and the adoptive parents' ability to meet their child's needs.

Birthparents who so wish are often given a description of the adopting parents. Margaret Trowbridge, a birthparent relinquishing her son for adoption, received a sketch of her son's perspective adoptive parents. An excerpt of the description follows:

> Mrs. N., thirty-one, and Mr. N., thirty, are Caucasians and members of a Protestant church. They own their own home and both are professional people. They are unable to have birthchildren and wish eventually to adopt two children. Mrs. N. plans to leave her job when they adopt a child. She is particularly close to her own family, who live in the area. Mr. N. has an active interest in the outdoors.

Laurel and John Newman, the adopting parents described above, also received a description of Margaret Trowbridge and her son's father, Dick LaBelle. An excerpt of the material presented to the Newmans follows:

> Miss T.: The birthmother is a twenty-seven-year-old, Caucasian, attractive, blue-eyed, dark-haired woman. She is college-educated and employed as a technical advisor. She comes from a wealthy Protestant family an believed that a child resulting from a nonmarital relationship would not be accepted by her family or friends.

> Mr. L.: The birthfather is a college instructor in his late twenties. He is Jewish and has blue eyes and red hair. Mr. L. is planning to marry a woman other than his son's mother.

These descriptions were given in verbal form to the adopting parents in order to provide them with information about the child they were considering adopting. After their acceptance of the child, the agency presented the Newmans with nonidentifying written descriptions of the birthparents to give to their adopted child.

Most agencies will share this nonidentifying information at the time of the adoption and afterwards upon the requests of birthparents, adoptive parents, and adoptee. However, this is shared at the discretion of the agency. Again, identifying information is only released under court order. (See Chapter Five for a detailed discussion.)

The Attorney's Records

Most attorneys will keep records of the adoptions they handle. Usually attorneys for nonagency adoptions will have the names of the birthparents, their addresses at the time of the adoption, and the circumstances leading to the adoption within their records. When attorneys have acted as intermediaries — the arrangers of adoptions — their records may be more complete. (Refer to Chapter Six for further discussion.) The attorney for an agency adoption generally has little information of interest to the adoptee.

Confidentiality is usually less protected in nonagency adoptions, in which attorneys play such principal roles. This is a result of the process rather that the actual wishes of the parties involved. Most states require the birthparent to participate in the placement process and often to make the placement herself. The birthparent usually signs a written consent for her child's adoption by specific persons. Usually the birth and adoptive parents and the attorney retain a copy of this consent.

The information an attorney possesses concerning an adoption is protected by attorney-client privilege. The consent of the attorney's client — whether adoptive parents, birthparents, or both — is needed in order for the adoptee to receive information.

The Court Adoption Records

Adoption proceedings for children are private. Only court personnel, the parties to the adoption, their attorneys, and a representative of the investigatory agency usually attend. As part of these proceedings the court collects information and records. Among the court records relevant to the background of the adoptee are:

- a transcript of the proceedings
- the original birth certificate
- the relinquishments or consents of the natural parents
- the report and recommendations of the investigatory agency
- the adoption petition
- the adoption decree

Once the adoption is final these records are permanently sealed. A copy of the adoption decree is then available. However, the names of the natural parents and the original name of the adoptee are deleted.

Usually these records are available only to the attorney for the adoption, the adoption agency, and under some circumstances the adopting parents. Others can obtain access to these records only by court order.

The Exceptions

Five states — Alabama, Kansas, South Dakota, New Jersey, and Minnesota — differ from the national pattern of total and permanent confidentiality of the records.

Alabama. Alabama allows adult adoptees born in Alabama access to their original birth certificates. In 1977 Alabama set up a state registry to handle adoptees' requests.

Kansas. Kansas allows adult adoptees (or their guardians if they are still minors), and other parties with a direct interest, access to the original birth certificates. Birth certificates are available through the state clerk of vital statistics.

South Dakota. South Dakota's adoption and confidentiality laws are basically similar to those of the majority of other states. However, the codes make *no* provision for the sealing of the original birth certificates. Adoptees born in South Dakota may be able to secure their original birth certificate because of the omission of this provision.

New Jersey. New Jersey laws regarding the confidentiality of the records of adoptions are again similar to the majority of the states. However, a 1977 state court decision expanded New Jersey adoptees' access to information about their past. In response to this decision administrative policy established a state registry available to New Jersey adult adoptees, wards, foster children, and birthparents and foster parents interested in meetings. Interested parties should contact:

New Jersey Department of Institutions and Agencies
Division of Youth and Family Services
Box 510
Trenton, N.J. 08625

Minnesota. Minnesota is the first and only state to respond legislatively to the movement toward opening adoption records. In 1977 Minnesota enacted legislation providing adult adoptees with limited access to their original birth certificates.

Briefly, adoptees over twenty-one and born and adopted in Minnesota may make a written request for their original birth certificate to the Section of Vital Statistics. Included in the request should be the following:

- the adoptive name
- the birthdate
- the place of birth
- the names of the adoptive parents

Vital Statistics forwards this to the State Department of Public Welfare, which then refers the request to an appropriate local agency. The local agency then has six months to locate the birthparent or birthparents and to secure their consent for the release of the original birth certificate. After notice, the birthparent has four months to respond to the request. The consent of the birthparent is necessary for the release.

If the birthparent is deceased or refuses consent, Vital Statistics will inform the adoptee. The adoptee can still petition the court for the release of the birth certificate and Vital Statistics often assists in the process.

Interested persons should contact:

Section of Vital Statistics
717 Delaware, S. E.
Minneapolis, Minn. 55440

Minnesota's program has been a remarkable success. In its first year of operation 340 adoptees requested their birth certificates. Currently, Vital Statistics receives approximately thirty requests a month. In 75 to 80 percent of the cases the birthparents have been located or found to be deceased.

Why the Search?

Most of us at some time in our lives have wondered about our origins and our roots. We ask our grandfathers to tell us stories of the old country, our parents to tell us of their childhoods, and perhaps pay a geneologist to trace our family tree. Our histories are an interesting curiosity and, more importantly, part of our identities. Adoptees, too, feel this same natural curiosity about their historical and biological roots.

Some adoptees are content to have background information about themselves and knowledge of the reasons for their adoptions. Others, however, wish to actually meet, talk with, and perhaps have a relationship with their birthparents. Several studies indicate that the more information adoptees are given as children about their birth heritage, the less likely they are as adults to seek out their birthparents.

Adoptees are individuals and have their own reasons for wanting a better understanding of their origins. However, some of the more common reasons adoptees search for more information about their birth heritage are:

- identity concerns
- a desire for medical and genetic information
- difficulties in their relationship with their adoptive family

Identity Concerns

Each of us develops a personal identity — a sense of who we are — from our biological heritage, our experiences, and our history. This sense of ourselves affects our success in our daily lives and our relationships with our friends and family.

Usually, along with a healthy striving for independence, a search for identity is part of an adolescent's experience. However, most people reexamine and change their feelings about themselves at other major junctures of their lives, for example, at marriage, the birth of a child, or upon reaching middle age.

Adoptees have a complicated task in putting together their identity. As adoptees, they are different from their friends and even members of their own families. They have two sets of parents — birth and adoptive. Both are important to their identity. They are further troubled by the probable gap in their history and lack of personal contact with their birth background. The confidentiality that surrounds their adoption complicates searching for

their background, and causes them to wonder whether there is
something unacceptable about their background.

> Nineteen-year-old Tony is the now grown adoptive son of
> Laurel and John Newman. Tony is working and living away
> from home for the first time. He has a close relationship with
> his adoptive parents although he is careful to protect his
> independence. Tony knows the basic facts about his adop-
> tion but has begun to wonder about his birthparents. Are
> they still alive? Does he resemble them? Does he have
> brothers and sisters? And, most importantly, *why did they
> give him up?*

Tony, like most adoptees, feels a personal need to find out more
about himself. For him, this is not a rejection of his adoptive family but a healthy expression of his individuality and independence. As an adult he now lives apart from his family. As an adoptee he realizes that he is also biologically and somewhat histori-
cally separate from his family. The life, relationship, as well as his
separateness, are all part of his personal identity.

Medical and Genetic Information

> Ruth McFaddin is twenty-seven and recently married. She
> and her husband plan a family. Ruth is an adoptee. Her
> adoptive family received almost no medical information
> when they adopted the newborn Ruth. Ruth, and her hus-
> band too, wonder about her background and are concerned
> about the genetic heritage she will pass on to their future
> children.

Often an adoptee's marriage, pregnancy, or illness precipitate
an increased interest in his or her biological background. Recently agencies have recognized the importance of collecting and
forwarding an adoptee's medical and genetic background. However, many adoptees find themselves with a very sketchy medical
history. They are left concerned that their children will inherit
undiscovered genetic problems. Additionally, the adoptees
themselves are likely to be concerned that they have medical
problems of which they are unaware. For example, they may
wonder whether they should take extra precautions against heart
disease or diabetes.

Unsatisfactory Relationship with the Adoptive Family

> Carolyn Douglas, twenty-one, has lived separately from her
> adoptive family for the last two years. Her parents are now in

the middle of a bitter divorce. Carolyn feels the divorce was too long in coming. She can never remember her parents being happy. In fact, she does not remember herself being happy at home. Carolyn feels close to her adoptive father, but is now experiencing her adoptive mother as a distant and demanding woman. Perhaps with her "real" mother she could find a family.

Adoption provides no guarantee of a happy family life for the adoptee. Adoptees are as likely as anyone to experience troubled childhoods and difficulties with their parents. In fact, some studies indicate that adoptive families have *more* problems than the average family. The reasons for this are unclear. Perhaps the adoptive relationship and the adoptive experience produce additional strains. The preadoptive screening of prospective adoptive parents may be inadequate. Or the adoptive experience may make adoptive families more willing to seek help when they confront normal family problems.

Adoptees have an imaginary or perhaps even real resource in their birthparents when they experience difficulties with their adoptive families. As children they could only fantasize about their appearance, but as adults they may have the ability and the independence to seek out their birthparents.

These adoptees' need to search for their birth heritage is strong for several reasons. The unsatisfactory nature of their relationship with their adoptive families may make them all the more concerned with the reasons for their adoption. Feeling a mixture of anger and curiosity, they need to know what difficult circumstances made their birthparents surrender them to their adoptive families. They question whether the life their birthparents might have given them could have been better than their life with their adoptive family. These adoptees may also hope that a relationship with their birthfamily will replace the poor relationship they have with their adoptive family.

Help with the Search

Many adoptees *do* find more information about their background and often their birthparents in spite of the confidentiality surrounding the adoption process. The difficulties in searching for birthparents and the persistence of adoptees indicate the intensity of their need.

Among the resources used by adoptees in learning more of their biological heritage or in locating their birthparents are:

- their adoptive parents and families
- adoptee organizations
- adoption agencies (also see the section, "Access to Records")
- the courts
- vital statistics (also see the section, "Access to Records")

Adoptive Parents and Family

Often adoptees' best and beginning sources of information are their own adoptive parents. Many adoptive parents, as part of helping their children understand themselves, present them with all the information they know about their background. They may even know the names and past addresses of the birthparents and have many of the original adoption records if the adoptee was adopted independently. Some states allow the adopting parents, but not the adoptee, access to the court adoption records. Adoptive parents, by supporting their grown child's search, provide emotional acceptance for their child's actions, and allow agencies and attorneys to feel that they are not violating the confidentiality agreement made with the adoptive parents.

Adoptee Organizations

In recent years many adoptee organizations have been developed to help adolescent and adult adoptees understand their experience and search for their background. (The names and addresses of many of these organizations are listed in the appendix.) Usually these organizations have the following functions:

- providing adoptees with both emotional support and the opportunity to share experiences with other adoptees
- providing adoptees with practical assistance in searching for birthparents or information about the adoptee's background
- working to change the current confidentiality laws through education, media exposure, legislative lobbying, and court action

One of the more active of these organizations is Adoptees Liberty Movement Associates — ALMA (which means soul in Spanish). This movement was founded by Florence Fisher, herself an adoptee and the author of *The Search for Anna Fisher*. ALMA is a national organization with local chapters that is staffed by volunteer adoptees who have found their birthparents.

Another organization, Orphans' Voyage, was founded by Jean Patton, also an auther, to aid adoptees and other persons wanting to find their biological parents and families. This organization has also pressed for less confidentiality of the adoption records.

Adoption Agencies

Again, the original adoption agency may be able to provide nonidentifiable background information. Seldom will this information lead to finding an adoptee's birthparents. However, some adoptees find this information sufficient. Others can use this information as one step in their continued search.

The state department regulating adoptions is often a good referral source and may have a broader and clearer conception of the confidentiality laws than a local adoption agency.

☑ Reminder: New Jersey adoptees wanting information about or a meeting with their birthparents should contact the New Jersey Department of Institutions and Agencies.

The Courts

Most states provide for the opening of adoption records in exceptional circumstances. Persons having a direct interest in the adoption, such as the adoptees, adoptive parents, or natural parents, can ask the court to open or make available some portion of the adoption record. These persons must show the court that there is good cause or a compelling reason for opening the records. Whether good cause can be shown depends not only on the specifics of the situation but also on the interpretation of the judge and the state the action is brought in. When good cause is shown, the court will order all, a portion, or only personally nonidentifiable information to be released.

> A forty-seven-year-old adoptee was hospitalized for a serious, undiagnosed ailment. Her physician indicated that a complete family medical history was necessary for diagnosis and medical treatment. The court allowed this adoptee access to her adoption records.

> A twenty-eight-year-old adoptee was the parent of a mentally retarded son. She wanted a complete family an medical history in order to decide whether to become a parent again. She was given access to her adoption records.

An adoptee asked the court to open his adoption records. His psychiatrist indicated that he was deeply troubled by his lack of knowledge about himself, and that he felt there was something unacceptable about himself and his origins. In this situation some courts will allow an adoptee access to his records.

Adoptive Parents and the Search

The Newmans, the adoptive parents of nineteen-year-old Tony, are worried. Both have tried to reassure themselves that Tony's current interest in his birthparents is normal and no threat to their relationship with him. However, their intellectual acceptance of Tony's search does not stop their stomachs from churning or relieve all their worries. It is ridiculous, they know, but both wonder if they have failed as parents. Will their relationship with Tony be less close if he does find his birthparents?

The Newmans, like most parents of adult adoptees, worry about their child's search for his or her birthparents. Among the more common reactions of these adoptive parents are:

- fear that the birthparents will replace them
- wondering whether they have failed their child
- worry that their child will find his or her background unacceptable, the birthparents rejecting, or the experience upsetting
- anger at the adoptee for being interested in his or her birthparents
- anger at the birthparents
- fear that the adoptee will disrupt the birthparents' lives
- acceptance of the adoptee's need to search for the birthparents

Most adoptive parents find their feelings very mixed when they discover their child searching for his or her birthparents. Initially, they may be hurt and angry at this "ungrateful child" who is not content with the family they have provided. They may again recall the sadness they felt when they discovered themselves unable to have a natural child. Some may wonder whether they could have been better parents to their child.

Usually the relationship between the adoptive parents and adoptee is able to withstand the strain of the adoptee's search. When it does not, this is generally the result of an already poor relationship. Most often such a search indicates the emotional health of the adoptee and the adoptive parents' competence as parents. The adoptive parents have raised a child who feels able to be independent, curious, and develop his or her own identity.

The search by adult adoptees for their birth identity is another one of their developmental crises. They may want in this situation, as with past problems, to turn to their adoptive parents for help and support. When they do so, this is again a good indication of closeness, trust, and sound communication between adoptees and their adoptive parents.

The adoptive parents can be of great practical and emotional help in the search. Many adoptees are afraid of hurting their adoptive parents and as a result are reluctant to search for their birthparents or ask their adoptive parents for help. These adoptees often want their adoptive parents' permission before they search for their birthparents. As a practical matter, adoptive parents often have information, access to records, and abilities that will help their adopted child in the search.

Birthparents and the Search

Margaret Trowbridge Mills, Tony Newman's birthmother, is now forty-six years old. Mrs. Mills is married and the mother of a sixteen-year-old girl and a fourteen-year-old boy. Her husband knows of the son she placed for adoption nineteen years ago but her children do not. Mrs. Mills is satisfied that she made the best decision possible when she placed her infant son for adoption. However, she still thinks of this little boy and wonders how his life has turned out. She does not, however, have any plans to contact him.

Dick LaBelle, Tony's birthfather, never consented to Tony's adoption. Only recently has the consent of unmarried fathers been routinely required. Mr. LaBelle knew of Tony's adoption and, at the time, believed adoption was best for the boy, the mother, and himself. He has married twice but has never had any other children. Sometimes he thinks of the adoption with regret and wishes that he knew his boy. Mr. LaBelle also does not plan to contact his son.

Birthparents usually wish to have their anonymity protected immediately after placing a child for adoption. This was particularily true years ago when nonmarital pregnancies were much less acceptable. Confidentiality often allowed birthparents to put an unwanted pregnancy behind them and to continue with their normal lives.

In recent years many birthparents have become less concerned with confidentiality. They have matured and often view the placing of a child for adoption as only one among many of their usually happy and successful experiences. Some realize that their families and friends would now accept the child they surrendered for adoption. Most birthparents continue to feel concern for their children's welfare and are curious about how they are faring. (Refer to Chapter Ten for an in-depth discussion.)

Few birthparents actually search for their relinquished children. Often they indicate that the adoptive parents are the child's "real" parents and that they will do nothing to jeopardize or interfere with the functioning of the adoptive family. Many feel that they gave up all rights to having contact with their children when they placed them for adoption.

A 1976 California study revealed that the great majority of birthparents (82 percent) would meet with an adult adoptee if the adoptee desired. Only 5 percent were actually searching for the adoptee. Among the reasons given for meeting with the relinquished adoptee were:

- A meeting might help the adoptee.
- The adoptee might have a strong need to know.
- The birthparents' families could now handle a meeting.
- The birthparents feel a need to explain to the adoptee why he or she was given up for adoption.

When Birthparents Initiate the Search

Eighteen years ago Sandra Nelson placed her infant daughter for adoption. As the adoption was independent, arranged through an intermediary who was a mutual friend of Mrs. Nelson and the adoptive parents, Mrs. Nelson always knew her daughter's whereabouts. She wrote her relinquished daughter when the daughter was of legal age. Mrs. Nelson again described the reasons for the adoption, told the girl of her current life, ad let her know that she had a sixteen-year-old half-sister. Julie, her daughter, replied to the letter. She wrote Mrs. Nelson of the good life she had with her adoptive family and of her interests, and sent a photograph of herself. However, she ended the letter by saying that she did not want any future contacts.

Mrs. Nelson is the exception among birthparents who have relinquished a child. She knew her daughter's whereabouts, and she initiated contact. Increasingly, however, birthparents are attempting to contact their adult adopted children. Most of these birthparents recognize that they agreed to renounce all contact with their children. They are, though, joining adoptee groups, forming their own organizations, and pressing for the opening of the records.

The Reunion

Tony Newman did locate his birthmother, Margaret Trowbridge Mills, after five months' hard work, the assistance of his adoptive parents, and the help of an adoptee organization. He hesistantly phoned Mrs. Mills, and after the initial shock she agreed to join him for lunch. First they sized each other up physically and then very awkwardly began talking about the circumstances surrounding Tony's birth and adoption. Mrs. Mills described Tony's birthfather, Dick La-Belle, and explained how he might be located. They then began talking about their lives, their families, and their interests. After several hours they parted with no specific plans to meet again. Mrs. Mills felt relieved that Tony's adoption had worked out well. Tony felt he knew more about himself. Mrs. Mills told her husband about the meeting and Tony told his adoptive parents.

Neither Tony nor Mrs. Mills knew what to expect from the meeting. However, like many reunited adoptees and birthparents, both felt that many of their questions had been answered and that the meeting had relieved many of their worries.

Adoptees usually approach their birthparents with care and realize that the birthparents may not want the relationship to be openly acknowledged. Many adoptees only want more information and an explanation of why they were placed for adoption, not a continued relationship. Usually they are more concerned with the birthmother's explanation than with the birthfather's. Some adoptees are disappointed with the results of their search. They find their birthparents deceased, rejecting, or disturbed. However, even in these situations the adoptee generally feels better for having received the information rather than living with the unknown.

Most birthparents do not envision having a normal parent-child relationship with their adult adoptee. Approximately one quarter of such parents, according to a California study, indicate that a friendship relationship might be possible. Many, though, stress that the adoptive family is the adoptee's family. These birthparents state that they now have their own families and obligations and do not envision having a parental relationship with a child they relinquished so many years ago. Birthparents generally feel that meetings will be upsetting and for this reason favor social agencies acting as intermediaries in the process.

Toward an Opening of the Records

Adult adoptees are increasingly able to gain access to their own adoption records. This change in policy is not happening suddenly, only on one level, or consistently. Public exposure to the problems of the adoptee, as well as a change in social values, have influenced adoptees, birthparents, adoptive families, adoption professionals, legislators, and the courts. As a result, in an inconsistent and piecemeal fashion, adoption records are increasingly open to the adoptee.

Foreign Experiences

Since 1930 Scotland has allowed adult adoptees access to their adoption records. The effects of this Scottish statute were studied in 1974. The study indicated that the search was not vindictive but an attempt by the adoptees to better understand themselves. Many of the adoptees benefited from their search even when the information they uncovered was disturbing. On the basis of this report, England enacted legislation in 1977 giving adoptees over the age of eighteen access to their original birth certificates. In the same year a similar recommendation was made in Ontario, Canada.

Changes in Public and Professional Opinion

The publication of Jean Paton's *Orphan Voyage* and then in 1973 of Florence Fisher's *The Search for Anna Fisher* brought public attention to the identity searches of adult adoptees. Adoptees were no longer viewed only as infants placed in the arms of delighted childless couples but also as adults openly demanding the opportunity to make their own sense of their birth and adoptive heritage. As with many new concepts, this idea spread to professional groups and the media, and encouraged other adoptees and birthparents to voice their concerns.

Adoptees, birthparents, and adopted parents seem to support more openness in the adoption records. Another recent California study indicated that 89 percent of adoptees, 82 percent of birthparents, and 73 percent of adoptive parents support the right of adult adoptees to have access to their original birth certificates. Adoption agencies report a definite increase in interest in identifying information. Los Angeles County, for example, reported that in 1976, 247 birthparents and 278 adoptees contacted them for information regarding their records.

Adoption professionals are modifying their attitudes toward complete confidentiality of the adoption records. Adoption agencies now realize the importance of background information in the adoptees' process of forming their own identity. Most now provide adoptees and their families with substantially more information than they did in the past. Additionally, adoption agencies now often warn birthparents and adoptive parents that total confidentiality of the records cannot be promised in the future.

These changes in actual practice are reflected in national welfare and professional organizations. In 1977, the Child Welfare League of America (the largest private U.S. child welfare organization) revised its adoption standards. The organization reaffirmed the value of confidentiality to all parties to the adoption but at the same time urged agencies to advise their clients that such confidentiality cannot be assured in the future. Another major organization, the National Association of Social Workers, has advocated specific legislation giving adult adoptees more access to their records.

The legal profession also appears to be joining other professions in supporting the adult adoptee's right to know. In 1977, for example, the California State Bar Association announced support for legislation providing adult adoptees with limited access to identifying information.

The Courts

All states make a provision for the opening of confidential adoption records by court order. Generally good cause or compelling circumstances must be shown. (Five states — Alabama, Kansas, Minnesota, New Jersey, and South Dakota — also provide broader access.) Neither the state courts nor the U.S. Supreme Court have set aside these good cause statutes or established the adult adoptee's unconditional right to see the adoption records.

However, the courts have broadened their interpretation of good cause. In some cases the emotional needs of the adoptee were considered good cause for opening the records. A 1977 New Jersey state court decision gave an adoptee access to the records for these reasons and provided a state agency with justification for establishing a state registry for adoptees and birthparents. Also in 1977 a New York state court decision, appropriately named "In re Anonymous," granted an adoptee access to his adoption records for "mental rehabilitation."

Legislation

The process of change is also seen within the state legislatures. In 1977, Minnesota enacted legislation providing a mechanism for adoptees' to secure their original birth certificates. Similar legislation was introduced in California in the same year. It was approved by the legislature but vetoed by the governor. In 1978 the bill was reintroduced but eventually died. However, the legislature was confronted with a new and stronger bill in 1979. At the time of writing this bill is still being studied.

Appendix

Adoption Resources

State Agencies

The state agencies will provide listings of licensed adoption agencies within their state or direct you to an agency that will provide such a listing. These agencies are also a resource for current information regarding state adoption laws and procedures, foreign adoptions, child welfare services, adoption exchanges, and state and community adoption related organizations.

Alabama

Bureau of Family and Children's Services
State Department of Pensions and Security
Administrative Building
64 North Union Street
Montgomery, Alabama 36104

Alaska

Department of Health and Social Services
Pouch H-05
Juneau, Alaska 99811

Arizona

Department of Economic Security
P.O. Box 6123
Phoenix, Arizona 85005

Arkansas

Division of Social Services
Department of Social and Rehabilitative Services
P.O. Box 1437
Little Rock, Arkansas 72203

California

Adoption Services Section
Social Services Division
Department of Health
714 P Street
Sacramento, California 95814

Colorado

Division of Title XX Services
Department of Social Services
1575 Sherman Street
Denver, Colorado 80203

Connecticut

Department of Children and Youth Services
345 Main Street
Hartford, Connecticut 06115

Delaware

Division of Social Services
Department of Health and Social Services
Box 309
Wilmington, Delaware 19899

District of Columbia

Bureau of Family Services
Social Rehabilitation Administration
122 C Street, N.W.
Washington, D.C. 20001

Florida

Office of Social and Economic Services
Department of Health and Rehabilitative Services
P.O. Box 2050
Jacksonville, Florida 32203

Georgia

Division of Social Services
Department of Human Resources
47 Trinity, S.W., Rm. 211-H
Atlanta, Georgia 30334

Hawaii

Department of Social Services and Housing
P.O. Box 339
Honolulu, Hawaii 96809

Idaho

Department of Health and Welfare
Statehouse
Boise, Idaho 83702

Illinois

Department of Children and Family Services
623 E. Adams Street
Springfield, Illinois 62706

Indiana

Social Services Division
State Department of Public Welfare
1415 Meridian Street
Indianapolis, Indiana 46225

Iowa

Bureau of Family and Adult Services
Division of Community Services
Lucas State Office Building
Des Moines, Iowa 50319

Kansas

Division of Children and Youth
Department of Social and Rehabilitative Services
State Office Building
Topeka, Kansas 66612

Kentucky

Bureau of Social Services
Department of Human Resources
403 Wapping Street
Frankfort, Kentucky 40601

Louisiana

Division of Family Services
Health and Human Resources Administration
P.O. Box 44065
Baton Rouge, Louisiana 70804

Maine

Department of Human Services
State House
Augusta, Maine 04330

Maryland

Department of Human Resources
Social Services Administration
1315 Saint Paul
Baltimore, Maryland 21202

Massachusetts

Division of Family and Children's Services
Office of Social Services
Department of Public Welfare
600 Washington Street
Boston, Massachusetts 02111

Michigan

State Department of Social Services
300 South Capitol
Lansing, Michigan 48926

Minnesota

Department of Public Welfare
Centennial Building
St. Paul, Minnesota 55755

Mississippi

State Department of Public Welfare
Box 4321
Fondren Station
Jackson, Mississippi 39216

Missouri

Division of Family Services
Department of Social Services
Broadway Street Office Building
Jefferson City, Missouri 65101

Montana

Social Services Bureau
Department of Social and Rehabilitation Services
Helena, Montana 59601

Nebraska

Department of Public Welfare
1526 K Street, 4th Floor
Lincoln, Nebraska 68508

Nevada

Welfare Division
Department of Human Resources
251 Jeanell Drive
Capitol Mall Complex
Carson City, Nevada 89701

New Hampshire

Bureau of Child and Family Services
State Department of Health and Welfare
8 Loudon Road
Concord, New Hampshire 03301

New Jersey

Division of Youth and Family Services
Department of Institutions and Agencies
Box 510
Trenton, New Jersey 08625

New Mexico

Field Manager, Adoption Services
P.O. Box 2348
Santa Fe, New Mexico 87501

New York

Division of Services
New York State Department of Social Services
1450 Western Avenue
Albany, New York 12203

North Carolina

Children's Services Branch
Division of Social Services
Department of Human Resources
325 N. Salisbury Street
Raleigh, North Carolina 27611

North Dakota

Community Services
Social Services Board
Capitol Building
Bismark, North Dakota 58505

Ohio

Department of Rehabilitation and Welfare
30 East Broad Street
Columbus, Ohio 43215

Oklahoma

Division of Services to Youth and Children
Social and Rehabilitative Services
State Department of Institutions
P.O. Box 25352
Oklahoma City, Oklahoma 73125

Oregon

Adoption Department
Children's Services Division
Department of Human Resources
509 Public Service Building
Salem, Oregon 97310

Pennsylvania

Bureau Of Child Welfare
State Department of Public Welfare
Health and Welfare Building
P.O. Box 2675
Harrisburg, Pennsylvania 17120

Rhode Island

Child Welfare Service
Division of Community Services
600 New London Avenue
Cranston, Rhode Island 02920

South Carolina

Department of Social Services
P.O. Box 1520
Columbia, South Carolina 29202

South Dakota

Division of Human Development
Department of Social Services
State Office Building
Illinois Street
Pierre, South Dakota 57501

Tennessee

Social Services
Department of Human Services
State Office Building, Rm. 310
Nashville, Tennesee 37219

Texas

Division of Special Services
Department of Public Welfare
John H. Regan Building
Austin, Texas 78701

Utah

Division of Family Services
Department of Social Services
333 So. Second East
Salt Lake City, Utah 84111

Vermont

Division of Social Services
Department of Social and Rehabilitation Services
81 River Street
Montpelier, Vermont 05602

Virginia

Division of Social Services
Department of Welfare
P.O. Box K-176
Richmond, Virginia 23288

Washington

Department of Social and Health Services
P.O. Box 1788
Olympia, Washington 98504

West Virginia

Division of Social Services
Department of Welfare
1900 Washington Street, East
Charleston, West Virginia 25305

Wisconsin

Division of Family Services
Department of Health and Social Services
State Office Building, Rm. 300
1 West Wilson Street
Madison, Wisconsin 53702

Wyoming

Division of Public Assistance and Social Services
Department of Health and Social Services
Hathaway Building
Cheyenne, Wyoming 82001

Adoptee Organizations

The following are among the national organizations that provide services to adolescent and adult adoptees. These services may include (1) support groups composed of other adoptees, (2) assistance with an adoptee's search for his or her birthparents, (3) education of the general public, and (4) legislative efforts to change confidentiality laws. Adoptees should also consult the telephone directory and community agencies for referrals for local adoptee organizations.

ALMA (Adoptees Liberty Movement Associates)
P.O. Box 154
Washington Bridge Station
New York, New York 10033

Orphan's Voyage
c/o Jean Paton
Cedaredge, Colorado 81413

Inter-country Adoption Agencies

The following are among the reputable agencies providing inter-country adoption services in foreign countries. Check with your state agency regulating adoptions first, as the status of these agencies may have changed. Local adoption agencies may also provide inter-country adoption services.

Agencies Requiring Direct Applications

Bangladesh

Families for Children, Inc.
10 Bowling Green
Pointe Claire
Quebec, Canada H9S-4W1

Colombia

Fundacion Los Pisingos
Calle 13 No. 22-22
Apartado Aereo No. 4111
Bogota, D.E., Colombia

Greece

Metera Babies Centre
Agioi Anargyroi Atticus
Athens, Greece
(Through International Social Service — American Branch,
unless family is adopting in Greece.)

India

Holt Adoption Program, Inc.
P.O. Box 2420
Eugene, Oregon 97402
(In conjunction with Warne Baby Fold)

Kuan-Yin Foundation, Inc.
Barlanark RR #1
Burlington, Ontario
Canada

Missionaries of Charity
c/o Mrs. Aggarwal
11 Link Road
Jungpura Extension
New Delhi, India

Korea

Dillion Family and Youth Services, Inc.
2525 E. 21st Street
Tulsa, Oklahoma 74114

Friends of Children of Vietnam
600 Gilpin Street
Denver, Colorado 80218

Holt Adoption Program, Inc.
P.O. Box 2420
Eugene, Oregon 97402

Philippines

Holt Adoption Program, Inc.
P.O. Box 2420
Eugene, Oregon 97402
(Cooperatively with Holt Sahathai Foundation)

Agencies Requiring Referral From Local Adoption Agencies

Social Welfare Society, Inc.
Central P.O. Box 24
Seoul, Korea

International Social Services — American Branch
345 East 46th Street
New York, New York 10017

Adoption Requirements by State

These tables are for general reference. Adoption statutes are continually changed. Administrative procedures are also subject to frequent change. For specific questions consult your attorney or a licensed adoption agency.

Who May Adopt a Child

State	Single Persons	Married Persons	Married Person Alone	Residency Requirements	Comments
Alabama	Yes	Yes	No	No	
Alaska	Yes	Yes	Yes	No	Either of the unmarried natural parents may adopt.
Arizona	Yes	Yes	Yes	Yes	
Arkansas	Yes	Yes	Yes	No	
California	Yes	Yes	Yes	No	Adopter must be at least 10 years older than adoptee. An adult may not adopt his or her spouse.
Colorado	Yes	Yes	Yes	No	A person under 21 must have the approval of the court to adopt.
Connecticut	Unclear	Yes	Yes	No	Connecticut has a complex statute. Most adoptions take place under aegis of the welfare commissioner or adoption agencies.
Delaware	Yes	Yes	Yes	Yes	Petitioner(s) must be at least 21. Divorced persons may adopt.
District of Columbia	Yes	Yes	Yes	No	Petitioner may be a minor.

State	Single Persons	Married Persons	Married Person Alone	Residency Requirements	Comments
Florida	Yes	Yes	Yes	No	An unmarried minor natural parent may adopt. Homosexuals may not adopt.
Georgia	Yes	Yes	Yes	Yes	A single person must be at least 25. At least one of the petitioners must be an adult if the petitioners are a married couple. Petitioner(s) must be at least 10 years older than adoptee.
Hawaii	Yes	Yes	Yes	No	
Idaho	Yes	Yes	Yes	Yes	Petitioner must be at least 15 years older than adoptee or at least 25, unless petitioner is the spouse of the natural parent.
Illinois	Yes	Yes	No	Yes	Minor may adopt with court approval.
Indiana	Yes	Yes	Yes	Yes	
Iowa	Yes	Yes	Yes	No	
Kansas	Yes	Yes	Yes	No	
Kentucky	Yes	Yes	Yes	Yes	Petitioner must be at least 18.
Louisiana	Yes	Yes	Yes	No	Single persons must be at least 21.
Maine	Yes	Yes	No	No	Adopting parents must be of the same religion as natural parent(s) if specified and possible when adopting through the Dept. of Health & Welf.
Maryland	Yes	Yes	Yes	—	Petitioner must be at least 18.
Massachusetts	Yes	Yes		No	Petitioner must be older than adoptee and not his spouse, sibling, aunt or uncle.
Michigan	Yes	Yes	No	No	Michigan requirements are complex. Consult the statutes.

State	Single Persons	Married Persons	Married Person Alone	Residency Requirements	Comments
Minnesota	Yes	Yes	Yes	Yes	Residency waivable.
Mississippi	Yes	Yes	No	Yes	Residency waivable for relatives.
Missouri	Yes	Yes	Yes	No	Court may dismiss petition if spouse does not join.
Montana	Yes	Yes	Yes	No	Single petitioner must be at least 18. A married person, at least 18, may petition if separated from spouse. Either unmarried parent may petition to adopt his illegitimate child.
Nebraska	Yes	Yes	Yes	No	
Nevada	Yes	Yes	No	No	Petitioner(s) must be at least 10 years older than adoptee.
New Hampshire	Yes	Yes	Yes	—	The foster parent or unmarried parent of adoptee may petition.
New Jersey	Yes	Yes	Yes	No	Petitioner must be 10 years older than adoptee and at least 18.
New Mexico	Yes	Yes	Yes	No	Married petitioners may be minors.
New York	Yes	Yes	Yes	No	Unless the adoptee is the natural child of one of the petitioners, married petitioners must be adults.
North Carolina	Yes	Yes	Yes	Yes	Petitioner must be at least 18.
North Dakota	Yes	Yes	Yes	No	Unmarried parent of adoptee may petition.
Ohio	Yes	Yes	Yes	No	One of two unmarried petitioners must be an adult. An unmarried minor parent of adoptee may be the petitioner.

State	Single Persons	Married Persons	Married Person Alone	Residency Requirements	Comments
Oklahoma	Yes	Yes	Yes	No	Petitioner(s) must be at least 21 unless the unmarried natural parent of the adoptee.
Oregon	Yes	Yes	No	No	
Pennsylvania	Yes	Yes	Yes	No	
Rhode Island	Yes	Yes	No	No	Adopter(s) must be older than adoptee.
South Carolina	Yes	Yes	Yes	No	Regardless of age the unmarried parent of an illegitimate child may petition to adopt.
South Dakota	Yes	Yes	Yes	No	Adopter must be at least 10 years older than adoptee.
Tennessee	Yes	Yes	Yes	Yes	Single adopter must be at least 18 and a U.S. citizen, & one of two married adopters must be a U.S. citizen, unless adoptee is not a U.S. citizen. An unmarried mother may adopt her illegitimate child.
Texas	Yes	Yes	Yes	No	
Utah	Yes	Yes	Yes	No	
Vermont	Yes	Yes	No	No	Petitioner must be an adult & of "sound mind."
Virginia	Yes	Yes	Yes	Yes	
Washington	Yes	Yes	Yes	No	
West Virginia	Yes	Yes	Yes	No	
Wisconsin	Yes	Yes	Yes	Yes	When possible petitioners should be of the same religion as natural parents.
Wyoming	Yes	Yes	Yes	Yes	

Adoption State By State

State	Permits Independent Adoptions	Requires Accounting of Expenses	Access to Records Without Court Order
Alabama	Yes	No	Adult adoptees allowed original birth certificate
Alaska	Yes	Yes	No
Arizona	Yes	Yes	No
Arkansas	Yes	No	No
California	Yes	Yes	No
Colorado	Yes	Yes, only allows payment of attorney's fees	No
Connecticut	Yes, must be placed by parents, or relative	No	No
Delaware	No, adoption by step-parent or blood relative exempted	No	No
District of Columbia	No, as above	No	No
Florida	Yes	Any fee over $500 must be approved by court	No
Georgia	Yes	No	No
Hawaii	Yes	No	No
Idaho	Yes	No	No
Illinois	Yes	Only official agency shall receive fee	No
Indiana	Yes, with exception of step-parent or relative, official approval needed first	No	No
Iowa	No	No	No

State	Permits Independent Adoptions	Requires Accounting of Expenses	Access to Records Without Court Order
Kansas	Yes	No	Permits adult a-doptee and other parties with a di-rect interest access to original birth certificates
Kentucky	Yes, with permis-sion of Child Wel-fare Commission	No person other than licensed a-gency may charge fees	No
Louisiana	Yes	No	No
Maine	Yes	No	No
Maryland	Yes, placement must be made by parent or relative	Only allows pay-ment of legal and hospital costs	No
Massachusetts	No, adoption by relatives of blood or marriage ex-empted	No	No
Michigan	Yes, placement must be made by parent, relative, or guardian	No	No
Minnesota	No, children over 14 or being adopt-ed blood relative or step-parent ex-empted	No	Adoptees over 21 can secure original birth certificates with consent of na-tural parents
Mississippi	Yes	No	No
Missouri	Yes	No	No
Montana	Yes	No	No
Nebraska	Yes, placement must be made by parent	No	No
Nevada	No	No	No
New Hampshire	Yes	No	No
New Jersey	Yes, placement made by parents	No	State registry for adult adoptees and birthparents

State	Permits Independent Adoptions	Requires Accounting of Expenses	Access to Records Without Court Order
New Mexico	No, relatives and stepparents exempted	No	No
New York	Yes, placement by relative, parent, or guardian	No	No
North Carolina	Yes	Only agencies allowed to charge fees	No
North Dakota	Yes, placement by parents	No	No
Ohio	Yes, prior consent of court or welfare dept. needed	No	No
Oklahoma	Yes	No	No
Oregon	Yes, placement made by relatives	No	No
Pennsylvania	Yes	Yes	No
Rhode Island	Yes, placement made by parents	No	No
South Carolina	Yes	No	No
South Dakota	Yes	No	Law makes no provision for sealing of original birth certificate after adoption
Tennessee	Yes, placement made by parents	No	No
Texas	Yes	No	No
Utah	Yes	No	No
Vermont	Yes	No	No
Virginia	Yes, with exception of biological relative, stepparent or guardian, approval of Comm. needed first	No	No
Washington	Yes	No	No

State	Permits Independent Adoptions	Requires Accounting of Expenses	Access to Records Without Court Order
West Virginia	Yes	No	No
Wisconsin	Prior approval of court needed	No	No
Wyoming	Yes	No	No

Glossary

adoptee: an adopted child or adult

adoption: a legal and emotional process by which a child becomes the child of parents other than his or her birthparents; the child and the adoptive parents then have substantially the same mutual rights and responsibilities as those which exist in the birthparent-child relationship

adoption agency: a licensed public or private agency that is authorized by law to accept children for adoptive placement, to select adoptive parents, to place children in adoptive homes, and to supervise children until their adoption is final

adoption subsidy: financial or medical assistance or both provided to children in order to facilitate their adoption; eligibility requirements and types of subsidy vary from state to state (See Appendix)

adoptive parent(s): the parent(s) of an adopted child or adult

adoptive placement: the placing of a child in the home of prospective adoptive parents for the purpose of adoption

birthparent(s): the biological parents of a child; also called *natural parents, biological parents,* and *real parents*

black market adoption: the illegal placement of a child with adoptive parents for profit

consent: the voluntary agreement of a parent to the legal termination of his or her parental rights

custody: the legal responsibility for the care and control of a child

dependent child: a child in the custody of the court

foster parent(s): persons who care for a child who is not their birth or adopted child; a child is placed in their home usually for payment and at the request of the child's parents or guardian, a social agency, or the court

gray market adoption: a nonagency adoption in which adoptive parents pay some or all of the costs relating to childbirth and adoption; gray market adoptions are legal in most states

guardian: the person(s) having legal control of a child, the child's property, or both until he or she is an adult; unless they are deceased or the court orders differently, the parents are a child's guardians

hard-to-place child: a child who is not readily adoptable; often this is the result of the child's age, racial background, mental or physical health, or because the child is part of a sibling group

homestudy: an in-depth evaluation of a prospective adoptive parent's suitability as an adoptive parent

illegitimate child: a child born to unmarried parents; in many states this term is no longer used — *nonmarital* is substituted for illegitimate; generally these children are legally considered the same as children of married parents

intercountry adoption: the adoption of a child by parent(s) who reside in another country; also called *foreign adoption*

legal adoption: adoption sanctioned and made permanent by the court

nonagency adoption: the legal adoption of a child who was not placed with the adoptive parents by a licensed agency; also called *independent adoption, direct adoption,* and *private adoption;* in some states nonagency adoptions are not allowed

psychological parent: the person who by providing a child with day-to-day care becomes the primary person in a child's life; this term, originally coined by Goldstein, A. Freud, and Solnit in their book, *Beyond the Best Interests of the Child,* is now commonly used

relinquishment: parent's surrender or release of their parental rights to their child

relinquishment adoption: an adoption in which a parent surrenders a child to an agency for adoptive placement

special needs: a child's medical, physical, emotional, developmental, educational, or genetic condition that requires extra help from the adoptive parents, social agencies, and community resources

ward: a child in the custody of the court

Index